like a
lampshade
in a
whorehouse

Jeremy P. Tarcher/Penguin
a member of Penguin Group (USA) Inc.
New York

like a lampshade in a whorehouse

MY LIFE IN COMEDY

Phyllis Diller

with Richard Buskin

JEREMY P. TARCHER/PENGUIN
Published by the Penguin Group
Penguin Group (USA) Inc., 375 Hudson Street, New York, New York 10014, USA ·
Penguin Group (Canada), 10 Alcorn Avenue, Toronto, Ontario M4V 3B2, Canada
(a division of Pearson Penguin Canada Inc.) · Penguin Books Ltd, 80 Strand, London
WC2R 0RL, England · Penguin Ireland, 25 St Stephen's Green, Dublin 2, Ireland
(a division of Penguin Books Ltd) · Penguin Group (Australia), 250 Camberwell Road,
Camberwell, Victoria 3124, Australia (a division of Pearson Australia Group Pty Ltd) ·
Penguin Books India Pvt Ltd, 11 Community Centre, Panchsheel Park, New Delhi–110
017, India · Penguin Group (NZ), Cnr Airborne and Rosedale Roads, Albany, Auckland
1310, New Zealand (a division of Pearson New Zealand Ltd) · Penguin Books (South
Africa) (Pty) Ltd, 24 Sturdee Avenue, Rosebank, Johannesburg 2196, South Africa ·
Penguin Books Ltd, Registered Offices:
80 Strand, London WC2R 0RL, England

All photographs in this book are reproduced courtesy of Phyllis Diller.

Most Tarcher/Penguin books are available at special quantity discounts for bulk
purchase for sales promotions, premiums, fund-raising, and educational needs.
Special books or book excerpts also can be created to fit specific needs. For details, write Penguin Group (USA) Inc. Special Markets, 375 Hudson Street,
New York, NY 10014.

Library of Congress Cataloging-in-Publication Data

Diller, Phyllis.
    Like a lampshade in a whorehouse : my life in comedy / by Phyllis Diller with Richard
Buskin.
        p.   cm.
    ISBN 1-58542-396-3
    1. Diller, Phyllis.   2. Comedians—United States—Biography.   I. Buskin, Richard.
II. Title.

PN2287.D467A3 2005   2004058520
792.702'8'092—dc22

Printed in the United States of America
10   9   8   7   6   5   4   3   2   1

This book is printed on acid-free paper. ∞

BOOK DESIGN BY AMANDA DEWEY

To All Who Dream

"You think I'm overdressed? This is my slip. . . . No, I'm going to tell you the truth about what I'm wearing. I used to work as a lampshade in a whorehouse. I couldn't get one of the good jobs."

CONTENTS

A QUICK WORD . . .

It is not my intention to offend anyone, yet in the interests of truth I do, at times, overstep the bounds of good taste. For this I apologize, but if you smell, you smell.

Every person in this book, no matter how harshly treated, comes under my overall umbrella of love. Read it at your own risk.

Phyllis

like a
lampshade
in a
whorehouse

"SHOCKING, ISN'T IT?"

The time: 1958. The place: the Fontainebleau Hotel on Miami Beach, that fabulous 1,200-room playground to the stars. Many of them perform in its nightclub, La Ronde: Frank Sinatra, Jerry Lewis, Bob Hope—these are the *crème de la crème*, baby. After three years of clawing my way around the discovery club circuit I've been hired to open for Big Band singer Don Cornell. It is, I feel sure, my big break; the catapult towards fame, money in the bank, peace of mind, being on everyone's A-list. Instead it's a big bust, the lowest point of my career. I'm fired after the first show.

To start with, the microphone gives me hell, cutting in and

out. And for another, I don't get a whole load of laughs, so I'm in a state of sheer panic. Oh, *Jesus*. Normally, I wear a chic little Chanel suit that exposes my legs and enables me to adopt a gan-gly stance that matches my disjointed face: a bent cone for a nose, no upper lip when I smile, and teeth like crooked tomb-stones. *Boy, am I ugly.* In this case, however, taking my lead from the female singers whom I've seen working hotel ballrooms, I buy a long gown and it's a bad move. Here I am, joking about life as a lousy, unattractive housewife, and I look more like some ditzy society hostess. It blows my entire act.

You know what keeps me humble? Mirrors! I considered chang-ing my name when I entered show business, but with a face like this, who cares? Just when I lost my baby fat, I got middle-age spread. I didn't have a good five minutes.

Unaware that the Fontainebleau's owner wants me out of there, I climb back into the Chanel suit and do a second show, but he never sees it. The next day I'm on a plane back to New York, forced to reunite with a deranged, unemployable husband in a scuzzy Greenwich Village hotel room where I cook our meals on a hot plate and wash our dishes in the john. Forget all the dreams, all the hopes for a better future. With no home, no bookings, and zero cash to pay the $60 weekly rent for this stinking dump, I have to borrow from our eldest child who sweeps away cock-roaches at an L.A. supermarket in order to finance his studies. It's just a pity he can't reach all the way to St. Louis, where cockroaches share an apartment with my in-laws and our four other kids, one of whom is schizophrenic.

Oh yeah, I'm doomed. And the Miami firing feels like the end, yet it turns out to be an ill wind that actually blows me some good.

I'll never look back.

One

THE FUNERAL-OF-THE-MONTH CLUB

I n the fall of 1934, I arrived at Chicago's Sherwood Conservatory of Music to study piano, voice, harmony, and theory. Just seventeen years old, I was a model of wide-eyed naiveté. I'd be well into my seventies before that would change.

Residing in a North Side apartment that had a fine grand piano on which to practice, I earned my room and board by serving as the governess of a little fella named Herbie Loseff. Herb's mother, Bessie, was studying to be a pharmacist, while his father, Sam, who already was a pharmacist, had some woman knocked up and in the hospital. He and another guy had both been screwing her—I suppose they were sharing the expense—but that evidently wasn't enough because the sonofabitch tried to rape me. He was a stumpy, revolting little bastard, and one morning as I was making the bed, he picked me up and began massaging my tits.

While he was titting me, I kept going on about his wife: "Just wait until I see Mrs. Loseff! If you don't stop, I'm going to tell her about this! Oh-ho, Mrs. Loseff *won't like it!*" Sweating like the pig that he was, Stumpy Sam didn't say a word, but after about a minute of me trying to squirm loose he suddenly saw sense and gave up. That was a pretty terrifying experience. I was still a virgin and I was really shaken up. However, when I called my parents and asked what I should do, their response was that I should do nothing. *Nothing.* Otherwise I'd have to talk to his wife and cause a whole upset.

Welcome to my world.

Right from the start my parents had left me to fend for myself. Apparently unaware that I was a kid, they invariably treated me like an adult, perhaps because they themselves were no spring chickens and perhaps because they'd never planned on having me in the first place. Indeed, when my mother missed a couple of periods and visited the Lima, Ohio, office of a Dr. Cavanaugh one icy-cold morning in November 1916, a cursory examination prompted the good doctor to conclude, "You have a tumor." A few days later she visited Lima Hospital to have it removed, and my father went along to watch—this was before television, so he didn't have anything else to look at.

"What's the excitement? Oh, an operation!"

"What do you want? A tonsillectomy?"

"No, I think I'll watch the tumor . . ."

So, my father was in the operating room when Dr. Cavanaugh opened up my mother and said, "Uh, it's a kid. This tumor has legs, arms . . . *ugly*-looking little thing!" Daddy was a really precious, darling man, and when the doctor asked him what should be done, he said, "Leave it in." Thanks to those three short words, I was born at home on newspapers about eight months later and christened Phyllis Ada Driver. (I still have a story on my butt, although now the print is much larger.)

You see, contrary to a widespread misconception, I am *not* Jewish. Diller (unlike Driver) is, for the most part, a Jewish name, many comics are Jewish, and at the start of my career I performed a huge number of Jewish benefits—since everyone assumed I was a Jew I'd always try to pass myself off as one . . . until they would ask what synagogue I belonged to, and then I'd be up the creek. I'll never forget when I performed a benefit in Pittsburgh and was given the most beautiful set of eight tiny sterling-silver cups. I've since discovered these were for *Kiddush*—for the wine to be drunk with Sabbath dinner—but back then I didn't have a clue. As far as I was concerned, they could have been for washing my eyes.

On the day of my grand entrance into this world, July 17, 1917, Britain's royal household changed its name from Saxe-Coburg-Gotha to Windsor. Not only was the old moniker a mouthful, but worse still it was German, and this was at a time when the Hun wasn't exactly leading Europe's popularity polls. A little over three months since President Woodrow Wilson had declared America's involvement in World War I, it was fortunate that my own family's surname didn't betray our ethnic roots. Instead, the tumultuous events of that year, ranging from Mata Hari's execution to Russia's Bolshevik Revolution, just seemed to pass us by.

Daddy was a balding guy of fifty-five when I was born, Mother was a gray-haired woman of thirty-eight, and all of my relatives were *old*. The "uncles" on my mother's side were actually my great-uncles, and while all of the aunts and uncles on my father's side were my real aunts and uncles, they were ancient—Daddy's eldest brother, Sam, had fought on the Confederate side in the Civil War, for chrissakes! My parents were forever taking me to funerals because their siblings were all dying. We belonged to the Funeral-of-the-Month Club.

I'm from such an old family, it's been condemned. I am descended from a very long line my mother once foolishly listened to.

In our family's case, the Driver surname was a derivative of Treiber. My great-great-grandfather, Ludwig Treiber, didn't want to join the German Army—and who can blame him?—so he sailed for America and landed in Philadelphia on October 17, 1749. There he changed his name to Lewis Driver, married Anna Barbara Sprenkle, and, like numerous other German settlers of that era, moved from Pennsylvania down to Rockingham County, Virginia, in the heart of the Appalachians. Nestled between the Blue Ridge mountains to the east and Allegheny Ridges to the west, Rockingham sits in the Great Valley where the Shenandoah River flows along the eastern side of the mighty

Peaked Mountain. A couple of centuries later, I'd buy a house on South Rockingham Avenue in Brentwood, California, but that (together with my DNA) is pretty much the extent of my genealogical connections.

The fifth of Lewis and Anna Driver's seven children was my paternal great-grandfather, Peter. He married one Dorothy Meyer, and the younger of their two children was my grandfather Benjamin. He was born exactly one hundred years before me. Ben and Dorothy had six boys and six girls, and my daddy, Perry M. Driver, was born second-to-last, in 1862. His middle name was just an initial—he'd later change this to Marcus.

As farmers in Rockingham County, the Drivers weren't rich but they also weren't dumb. They were solid, solid people, and the house that they built and all lived in is still standing. My father was very proud of saying, "I plowed a straight furrow." That's how he and his family were—they cared about what they did and they were honest. Years later, Daddy would reminisce about how they made their own clothing, how their mattresses were stuffed with straw, and how, with no running water, they would have to break the ice outside in the freezing cold of winter just to wash their faces. It was a different era.

My father attended the local school where his sister Elizabeth taught, and he stayed there through eighth grade—if anything went wrong in her class, he got it, because she didn't want to appear partial to her little brother. Growing up to be a handsome, curly-brown-haired man of about five feet eleven, he was a dandy, a beautiful dresser without an ounce of fat on him, and he had great physical coordination—at age seventy, he'd bowl 299 (the 300th pin would wobble but refuse to die)—and this bodily skill would be passed down to my children Perry and Stephanie, both of whom excelled at sports. At one time, my dad was an armed sheriff on horseback in Rockingham County; and his reputation was that "Driver shoots to kill," so he never had to shoot. I don't know how he earned that reputation—he was probably his own best press agent. However, it was in insurance sales that he eventually chose to pursue a career.

My mother, Frances Ada Romshe, was the daughter of John Romshe—more German blood—and a redheaded Irish firecracker named Frances Sellers. Mother had three older brothers: Loy, Clem, and Al, who were reduced to two when Loy fell out of a horse-drawn buggy and punctured a lung. Before long, my grandfather ran off and ended up having five wives—I guess if a girl leaned over a bed, he *shtooped* her. That left my grandmother with three children and the necessity to make a living, which in those days wasn't easy for a woman. Fortunately, however, she was a schoolteacher, so she bought a home next to a boys' school in Lima and helped make ends meet by housing and feeding the students.

At some point, Perry Driver called the house to make a date with a girl who was working for my grandmother, but Mother answered the phone and that was that. He never got away. She had the most fabulous voice, so warm and dramatic that it just drew you in, and it obviously did the trick on him—I know she wanted to be an actress. She played a couple of amateur roles in Lima, including that of Carrie Nation, the hatchet-wielding destroyer of booze joints who belonged to the Woman's Christian

Temperance Union. Years later, I'd play the same role on my NBC TV variety show.

Mother was a teetotaler, and although Daddy drank whiskey and smoked cigars when she first met him, that soon changed. She was *dominant*. In fact, when the two of them began dating, she told him, "Either this is going somewhere or I don't see you anymore." That's why they got married, eight years before my birth.

I was the world's ugliest baby. When I was born, the doctor slapped everybody. My father asked the doctor, "Is it a boy or a girl?" The doctor said, "No." He said it was the first full-term miscarriage he had ever witnessed. I was thirty years old and my mother was still trying to get an abortion.

Mother wanted everything her way because she was convinced that her way was best. She wanted to run everything and pretty much did. Still, Daddy wasn't submissive, so he and Mother would always argue until she wore him down. And if she didn't, she would go and visit a relative for a couple of days. That happened throughout my childhood. Daddy and I would be left to ourselves whenever she took off, and he'd be so down. At other times, when she got real mad at him, she'd go in the bedroom, shut the door, and sing hymns.

You see, not only could Mother play the piano and sing, but she was also a fanatical Protestant who believed every word of the Bible as written. If it said Jonah was in a whale, then kiddo, he was in a whale. Even as a child I couldn't buy that, and neither could my father. Nevertheless, what those two had was a love affair—believe me, they were meant for each other. They both had the same kind of work ethic and pride in what they did, they were both very, very bright, and they also had a terrific sense of humor.

I'm a combination of the two, having inherited my mother's fiery nature as well as her frugality. She was so frugal, most of my clothes were either hand-me-downs or homemade—fortunately, she was a fine seamstress. She made her own housedresses and did all her own housework, even though she was plagued by rheumatoid arthritis since the age of twenty. Her hip rheumatism was so bad that many people considered her a cripple, but that never entered my head. They'd say she had a gimpy leg—and she did have one leg shorter than the other—but she was always running, so you couldn't tell.

For his part, Daddy was a quiet, gentle soul with great social skills and a terrific personality. People adored him. Those were the days when a handshake was a contract, and he was honest. This is what I inherited from him, in addition to being a people person. I'll never forget the day I was with him on the street as a little kid, and he had a long conversation with some guy. Afterwards I asked, "Who was that?" and he said, "I have no idea." Years later, Bob Hope and I were standing on a street in Burbank and we were talking to someone who turned out to be a total stranger. Afterwards I said, "I thought he was *your* friend." Neither of us knew the man, but we'd both just stood there, wailing away. It was the same deal. Like my father, I have a sliding personality, where I can talk to the President or a bum and everybody in between. It's a wonderful thing.

When my parents were first married, Daddy commuted between the Lima office of the National Life Insurance Company of Montpelier, Vermont, and a dear little bungalow that he'd bought way out in the sticks. He left Mother there to sit outside and watch the squirrels and rabbits all day, but that wasn't for her. Besides, she also didn't trust what he might be getting up to at work. So, she saw to it that they traded the bungalow for a fifty-five-acre farm within the Beaverdam city limits—or make that village limits, because there were only nine hundred inhabitants—while renting an apartment nearby in downtown Lima to house both them and his office. That way she didn't have to worry about a secretary hitting on him. Instead, she became the secretary and bookkeeper, and from then on the routine was that she'd do the books and have a migraine.

Not that Mother had things all her own way. Located at the junction of the Lincoln and Dixie national highways, the Beaverdam property had seven beautiful oak trees, so she wanted to call it the Seven Oaks Farm, yet the name that ended up being emblazoned across the barn in huge letters was the P. M. Driver National Highway Farm. This was run by a neighbor, Mr. Reigle, whose colorful language concerned my parents when I was around, and who oversaw the raising of cattle and sheep for the market.

Shearing and lambing were times filled with excitement for me, and one of my fondest memories is of an operatic concert that I performed for those sheep one sunny afternoon when I was about five years old. Sheep are a great audience, they love music, and the whole flock faced me and was transfixed by my high soprano and strange language. In the Bible it's referred to as "speaking in tongues," and in this case it certainly was unintelligible not only to the listeners but also to the singer. I made it all up, yet it was very dramatic and the sheep just couldn't get enough.

Once a year we'd have "farm day," when my parents would play their part in the threshing process with a couple of mules named Fanny and Queen. How can I ever forget the sight of my little mother leading one of those strong, stubborn creatures by the nose? Never mind that she was five feet tall with a gimpy leg—nothing could hold *her* down. She loved it there, and so did my dad, whose astute farming sensibility stemmed from growing up in the Shenandoah Valley of, as he called it, "Ol' Virginny." Strolling in the great outdoors, he'd sometimes forget about the butting instincts of our one male sheep, Fifty-Four, and have to bolt over a fence in order to save his beautiful ice-cream suit. Daddy, you see, was never out of that suit, for it was in Lima that he made his living and where we spent all of our time.

Situated in northwestern Ohio, within a fertile farm area on the banks of the Ottawa River, this was a city with all the characteristics of a moderately sized, early twentieth-century Midwestern town: a population of just over 40,000; industry that revolved around lumber, oil, and the manufacturing of motor trucks; and a downtown area that basically consisted of a large square where Main and Market streets crossed, alive with the clanging sounds of Ohio's first electric streetcar system. I have such wonderful memories of traveling on those vehicles with their woven wicker seats and heavy metallic smell.

My entire childhood was spent in a couple of downtown apartments there, located a half-block from one another, and in each case it was the same deal: the front room was my father's office and the remainder was where we lived. The first place was located on the ground floor of the Electron Building at 210 Market Street, where my initial bed was a drawer and my earliest memories are of my mother placing me on a pillow in a corner of the living room and saying, "Now, don't you move. I'm going out, but you stay right there." And that's what I did.

I was breast-fed until I was two. When I started asking for it by name, my mother felt it was time to quit.

The building next to the Electron was a handsome eight-story structure of white tile that boasted just enough iron ornamentation to make it pretty. This housed the City Loan Bank, founded and owned by the Schoonovers, who made a fortune charging 20 percent interest; the upscale Thomas Apartments; numerous offices; and, somewhat incongruously, a grocery and meat market on the ground floor that provided me with two invaluable experiences very early on. Namely, thievery and frustration.

My mother would send me to that store before I could talk. I'd knock on the front door, a storekeeper would let me in, I'd hand him a shopping list as well as a purse with some money, and then return home with a few small items. Well, one day Mother kept sending me and I kept returning empty-handed. So, baffled and irritated, she finally went to see what was wrong and discovered that the place was closed. That's how she gave a two-year-old independence: if she told me to sit, I sat; if she sent me to the store, I went. This ability to take direction would be a great showbiz asset.

Following a long, cold, dull Ohio winter, the advent of certain seasonal fruits and vegetables was ample reason for excitement. Cantaloupe, watermelon, corn, tomatoes—all celebratory foods, with strawberries topping the list. So it was that, when some of those red, heart-shaped beauties were displayed on the sidewalk in front of the store, little Phyllis figured no one would notice if a couple disappeared. . . . Wrong. To this day I don't know who squealed (maybe my evil twin), but I was psychically arrested and handcuffed by Perry and Ada who delivered a stirring lecture on honesty. Then came the clincher: I was to return the two strawberries I'd stolen and apologize profusely to the store manager.

Armed with a couple of berries out of a box that my folks had bought to cover the store's loss, I duly gave my heartfelt speech and have never been tempted to steal *anything* since. (Hotel amenities don't count—shower caps are quite handy for covering bowls of food, and years of travel have left me with enough shampoo and lotion to float the *Queen Mary*.)

When a Japanese restaurant took over the ground floor of the Electron, we moved up to the second floor. However, that restaurant was always getting robbed, and one night some thieves also blew the safe of the bank next door; so, after that, I was afraid they were going to blow the safe and then come and get me while

I was alone. Just two years old, I was scared to death of everything because my mother taught me fear. She was only trying to protect me—she warned me about people who kidnapped children and this was very important—but I lived in total fear.

There was no such thing as preschool in those days, so from the age of two I was sent on the road with my father, sometimes even making night calls with him. Not until much later did I realize that Mother was constantly sending me away. It's called babysitting. She was crazy about me, but I don't think she wanted a child. Remember, my father was the one who had told the doctor to "Leave it in." He would put a small towel rack in front of the passenger seat of his old sedan and tell me to "Hold tight" when we went around corners. People thought I was his grandchild.

Daddy was a car person. His first vehicle was a right-hand-drive Paige, and after that I remember traveling in an Overland, a Gray-Dort, and then a Jewett sedan all over a large client territory in northwestern Ohio, including Lima and towns like Wapakoneta, Delphos, Findlay, Bluffton, and Beaverdam. We were one of the first families in Lima to have a vehicle, and when Democratic Presidential candidate William Jennings Bryan came to town, campaigning for abundant silver currency to replace the more exclusive gold standard, our Paige transported him in the parade. That was a big deal for a town like Lima, where the only summer entertainment was the circus, parades, and, once a year, chautauqua. (In the old days, this was an educational gathering that offered lectures, concerts, and theatrical performances.)

On the road, I observed my father's sales pitch. It was a concise, magnificently timed routine with a start, middle, and end, and he'd explain to me that, once you've finished your pitch, shut up. Don't say another word. Let the other person think. As a child, I heard his spiel over and over again. Dealing with farmers out in the field, he'd walk right up to their plows or tractors and ask them to "think about your wife being left with the farm." Referring to death as "an eventuality," he'd advise them to invest in life insurance as a means of financial support, and then, in a highly dramatic gesture, he would fan out a deck of cards containing the names of each of his policyholders; a big rainbow of happy customers. Oh boy, was he slick, and excepting a couple of years during the Great Depression, he was extremely successful within the modest confines of the world in which he operated.

I loved spending time with my dad and I'm sure he felt the same about me, but neither he nor my mother were the kind of people to sit me on their laps and give me a hug. Ours was a family of handshakers. There was no clutching or kissing, and the only time I ever saw my parents kiss was when Daddy was on his way to the hospital for a prostate operation. Heaven forbid there should be anything physical. Consequently, I myself would find it difficult to touch anyone until marrying my second husband, whose warm, boozy, Irish relatives were always clutching and kissing. That would encourage me to work at it, but close contact still doesn't come naturally. It drives me *nuts* that all I have to do is put my hand out and, before I know it, I'm enveloped, with someone biting my neck or blowing in my ear. Oh, *brother*. Even my cat doesn't want to be hugged.

When you play spin the bottle, if they don't want to kiss you they have to give you a quarter. Well, hell, by the time I was twelve years old I owned my own home.

I have a theory there's no such thing as a happy childhood. You don't own anything, you're not in charge of anything, and you have to take orders and do what you're told. There's just no freedom, and to make matters worse for me, Mother's frugality meant that I never had many toys or enough clothing. I hated that. Even back then I was clothes conscious. I was born clothes conscious. I didn't like my *diapers*. The only way I'd get party dresses was when they were on sale for five bucks at Flammer's, the one fashion store in Lima, so pre-school I'd use safety pins and old curtains to create my own designs.

Another thing I hated was not having my own bedroom. I always had to share with a roomer whose rent helped pay the bills. The second apartment where we lived was on High Street, above the office of Dr. Franklin Steiner, my father's dearest friend who owned the entire building. Dr. Steiner was rich; we were not rich, but it was signed in blood that nothing could be done to the apartment where we lived until after my father's death. In other words, he couldn't be put out for any reason whatsoever, and he never was. It was a true friendship.

Dr. Steiner had a small boy, also called Franklin, whom I insisted was my husband, and I dominated that poor little bastard. Oh, I remember it vividly: ordering him around in his sandbox, having him push the baby carriage around town with all my "children" in there, and my mother catching me answering the phone with an infant's voice and big-time attitude: "This is Mrs. Steiner." You see, I was already preparing for that life I thought I wanted, with a husband and lots of kids, and I was modeling our "relationship" on that of my parents. My dolls' names were Murphy, Josephine, and Phoebe, and to me they were *real*, because as an only child they made me feel wanted.

> *My parents had to tie a pork chop around my neck to make the dog play with me. . . . When I was kidnapped they wouldn't pay the ransom—they didn't want to break a ten. . . . I asked my mother how to turn off the electric fan. She said, "Grab the blade!"*

When I was really small, my father made me a sled, covered it in bunting, and he and Mother would pull me along at night, while I looked up at the stars and she pointed to the signs of the zodiac. I loved that. I also remember Mother and me going out on Halloween, attaching a dark piece of string to a purse, hiding in a bush, putting the purse on the sidewalk, and yanking it away when passers-by tried to pick it up. You see, we really did have a wonderful relationship, especially as I grew older, but she obviously didn't have time for little kids. And as I'm the same, I understand why she couldn't get me out of there quick enough.

Among the relatives, the only adult Driver who paid any attention to me was Aunt Eva, a sweet, soft-voiced little woman who never stopped smiling and who always wore a small bonnet. This matched the Amish-type clothing worn by her husband,

Sam, Daddy's white-bearded eldest brother who was a Dunker minister. (Dunkers belong to that group of German-American Baptists who baptize by total immersion and oppose military service and official oath-taking. Between them and my mother, it's hardly surprising I became an atheist.) Indoors the fashion code was thin, white cotton, outdoors it was black. Otherwise, I remember very little about Uncle Sam, a man seventy-five years my senior.

Most of the Driver family get-togethers were held at Uncle Al's house. He wore a raccoon coat and had a sonorous, booming voice that must have been a tremendous asset to his work as an outdoors auctioneer in the days before microphones. Al's wife, Aunt Hattie, was a tall, skinny, fearsome woman, totally gray in every way; gray hair, gray skin, gray legs, gray dress, gray voice. The two of them raised rabbits in their backyard. God knows why. They don't lay eggs, they don't do a damn thing except hump all the time. Still, I desperately wanted a rabbit, so my folks negotiated a couple for me and I collected them on my two-wheel sidewalk bike. After that we kept them in a large cage on the back porch and eventually we ate them. Hey, what else would you expect from part-time farmers?

At age six I began attending Franklin Elementary School. Since this was downtown, just a block away from our home, and most of the kids traveled there from the suburbs, I didn't have many neighborhood children to play with. Nevertheless, I'd go to the same building five days a week for the next twelve years because Central High was also located there. It was a fabulous, stately-looking, yellow-brick structure that took up an entire block, and I loved going there because I was surrounded by people. My first teacher was Alice Rossfeld, a dear, plump old maid who'd live to be ninety-six, but who was just a young woman when she took charge of me in first grade. I was the teacher's pet, and when I brought in a toy saxophone that I'd been given for Christmas, she put me on her desk and said, "Now, play for the class." She was always promoting my musical talent. Mother had pushed me up to the piano when I was still in my high chair, and since the age of three I'd been able to play in harmony. Just by hearing something I could play it.

In truth, I didn't have as much talent as my parents were led to believe—I was no Mozart. I just had a very good ear, and at age six I began formal piano lessons. Once a week, I'd get up a couple of hours before school and walk four blocks to the home of Mrs. MacDonald, a large, gray-haired woman who owned a floppy black spaniel that would sleep under the piano and snore while I played. What an audience. Yet, I loved it. From a very early age I pictured myself in the spotlight, sitting before a fabulous concert grand. That was my dream, and I'm sure it was also my mother's dream for me.

At first, I played an assortment of kiddie songs while listening to classical music. We didn't have a gramophone at home, but my father's sister Josina did. Her name was anglicized so that instead of being pronounced "Jo-seena" it was pronounced "Jo-syna," and everyone called her Sine, which to me sounded like something advertising Coca-Cola. She was a large woman with white hair and a typical Driver face—whereas the men were quite handsome, the women had long noses, and that's not pretty. Aunt Josina's daughter, Treva, had two little kids my age, so I spent a lot of time with that family. Again, my mother was taking advantage of any opportunity to send me away. She probably didn't know that Treva and her husband would sometimes take me for a drive around Lima, pass by the children's home, and joke that they might leave me there. I'd cry and they would laugh. Nice.

My folks took me to the children's home and told me to mingle. . . . When I was three, they sent me out for bubble gum, and while I was gone they moved!

Getting straight A's at school made me stand out, and so did Mother turning up when I was in Miss Bowsier's second-grade class and insisting that her child should sit on a pillow. Oh, *please.* The classroom had the usual wooden seats, I was the skinniest kid you've ever seen, and Mother thought that a full day of hard wood rubbing against those little bones would be too much. To tell you how skinny I was: there were nurses in grade school, and every time one of them took a look at me they'd send a note home saying, "Feed the kid." They didn't know my mother was a *terrible* cook. One time they even said, "Give her cream," but when Mother complied I broke out in a rash. The poor woman couldn't win.

In third grade, my teacher was Miss Tullis, a tall drink of water with no saving graces who embarrassed me twice in front of the class. I was not *her* pet. Having seen the silent 1925 movie version of *Ben-Hur* starring Ramon Novarro, I'd doused myself in an entire bottle of *Ben-Hur* perfume that had been handed out at the theater. Well, Tullis made me stand in front of the class before asking, "What is that stink?" and a short time later she roasted me again when I turned up with fur pinned around the bottom of my dress. Fur trim was all the rage that fall, but once more she stood me up in front of the kids and said, "What *is* that?" You see, I was way ahead, always interested in food and fashion, and for some reason that rancorous old witch tried to thwart me every step of the way.

In the summer of 1926, following the end of my third grade year, Mother conveniently decided it would do me good to be dropped off at the big working farm of her Uncle Charlie and Aunt Anna. Charlie had a couple of brothers, Justin and John, and they owned a place called Two Mile that provided each of them with two miles of fabulous farmland. Since Charlie was the wealthiest of the Romshes, my mother clearly knew what she was doing when she left me at his place. It was located about seven miles outside of Wapakoneta, the hometown of the first man on the Moon, Neil Armstrong, and my six-week stay on that farm probably aged everyone six years.

If ever there was a skinny little man who could only be described as vinegar it was Charlie, a real-life Scrooge who evidently hated children . . . or maybe just me. He always had a drop of water hanging off the end of his pointy nose and I don't believe he *ever* smiled. As my mother's favorite uncle he was my great-uncle, but he certainly wasn't great. He was an ugly little moth-eaten bastard.

Aunt Anna was fat and round, sweet and gentle; a prize-winning cook who baked pies, cakes, bread, cookies, and everything in between. Never have I tasted chicken, dumplings, mashed potatoes, and gravy that come close to hers—her chicken started in the coop and ended up on the chopping block. Now, that's *fresh.*

The farm measured nine hundred acres, with a fenced-in area at the front separating a great old house from the chicken yard, a shed that accommodated plows and farm machinery, and a huge two-story barn with horses on the ground level and hay up above. Indeed, most wonderful and fascinating to me were the animals: four dray horses, one carriage horse, six milk cows, calves, sheep, a collie named Scott, a mean, nasty-tempered little bulldog whose name I've forgotten, and cats and kittens who became my constant companions. What a thrill for a little kid starved for love and attention.

Everything on that farm ran like clockwork. There were three meals a day—eight a.m., noon, and five p.m.—and at five o'clock the cows were milked. At six, the milk went through a cream separator that made a rhythmic purring sound while squirting skimmed milk out of one faucet and pure cream out of another. The cream could be whipped or made into butter, and the cream separator was manufactured in Bluffton by a company named Readrite, owned by the father of one Sherwood Diller, whom I'd later marry. (Believe me, there's no shortage of *him* in this story.) At the time, however, I just wanted to be with Morris.

Morris was a hired hand with whom I fell madly in love. He lived "in" and actually farmed the entire nine hundred acres, and after Aunt Anna or her daughter Leona made his bed, I'd go into his room and fluff up the pillow . . . Oh honey, I'd do *anything* for him. I would peek longingly when he took his daily siesta on a day-bed in the living room. It lasted an hour. He, too, adhered to a strict routine.

Sunday featured church at noon and Monday was wash day, when some of the farm's most furious activity took place. Aunt Anna would fire up the great black iron stove that burned wood and heated gallons of water in great brass tubs. Bluing was then put into the water to make the sheets snowy white, and somehow, with all this primitive work going on, lunch was on the table at noon. We all ate. And Morris had his nap.

Tuesday was ironing day, while on Wednesday I'd sit in the cherry tree by the front gate and wait for the Huckster, a truck that brought manufactured products to the far-flung farms of Ohio. This included some much-needed candy, yet it was the ritual Saturday evening trip to Wapakoneta that inadvertently gave me a memory that I still clutch to my breast with honest reverence. Normally, Uncle Charlie and Aunt Anna would drive there in an old Pontiac, but one go-to-town night it wouldn't start, so we were transported in a clattering carriage pulled by a nervous, skittish horse whose rhythmic hoof-steps echoed the heartbeat of early American travel. I was in heaven. I can remember that carriage horse being tied up in front of the house and turning into a living cyclone when I threw a little water on him. Like me, he was probably starved for love and attention. I wish I knew then, as I do now, that you can talk to animals.

One of my major thrills was to collect eggs and throw grain to feed the chickens, and I also had a ball picking veggies for lunch or dinner. Green beans, peas, corn, asparagus, tomatoes, parsley, onions, and all sorts of edibles were grown in a large truck garden situated within the fenced-in area that accommodated the house. However, it was there, in the garden, that I indulged in a spot of youthful tomfoolery that forever reshaped my life, not to mention my poor, underprivileged face.

Mother was visiting the farm on that fateful day and she'd parked her Model T in the truck garden. I don't recall if we were heading into town, but at some point Aunt Anna climbed into the backseat, I got into the driver's seat, and I started the car. The vehicle was already in gear, and once it got going I couldn't get it to stop—only nine years old, I'd have to slide off the seat to reach those damned pedals. Instead, while Mother went into hysterics, I took my fat old aunt on the ride of her life, racing through the chicken yard and sending its inhabitants swirling into the air as I smashed through their feeders.

This farm, like many others, had a windbreaker consisting of fir trees lining the driveway, but I somehow veered off that drive way and swooshed under the trees. These were all that I could see on the windshield before the car hit the end of the driveway and slammed into a giant post. While poor Aunt Anna hit the back of my seat, the impact drove my face into the steering wheel and broke my nose. Needless to say, I was screaming, blood was everywhere, and pandemonium reigned. Yet, what was the first course of action? Well, my aunt and mother took me into the house, laid me on a couch, and placed a steak on my face. A *steak!* Since we were seven miles from the nearest town, this was the best they felt they could do, and the result was a disfigurement that ensured my already low self-esteem would become quite a bit lower.

Nobody ever told me I was ugly. I just didn't like my looks. I had that long Driver nose, and being broken meant that it was now nearly as crooked as my teeth. Since my parents didn't want to spend the money to get any of this fixed, and being that I never felt as well dressed as other kids, I had a major problem; a full-time complex that followed me around. It would be many, many years before I could rectify the situation, prolonged by the eventual realization that my looks were actually a formula for success. In the meantime I began compensating by way of two talents that would serve me well:

Musical ability and, apparent to all but me, an offbeat sense of humor . . .

Two

STANDUP NECKING

Entering fourth grade in the fall of 1926, my sole concerns should have been schoolwork, piano lessons, and playing with dolls. Yet, since the day my embryo had been mistaken for a tumor, my assigned role had been that of a drama queen, and at age nine this came into sharp focus.

Not only was my face a lopsided mess due to the runaway Model T fiasco on Great Uncle Charlie's farm, but for some reason my parents chose this as the time to inform me that Daddy had been married before and that I had a couple of half brothers. What a mindblower. I would never run into these step-siblings, and my father would never impart the details, but years later, long after my parents were gone, I'd be contacted by that side of the family and learn a little more.

Apparently, when Daddy was still living in Rockingham County he married one Adelaide Bowers, and together they had a son. Then, during her second pregnancy, she told him she was going to stay with her mother awhile, whatever that meant. They'd probably had a row. He said, "Either you come home with me or it's the end of this marriage," and she went for option number two. She resumed her maiden name and that was that. My father never saw any of them again. He was that kind of guy. His handshake was a contract, and so was his wave goodbye.

When I was eight, nine, ten, I watched Daddy suffer through several heart attacks with the doctor by his side, and he was in such pain that he would beg for a shot to put him away. He had angina pectoris, where a lack of blood to the heart causes severe chest pains. The medication prescribed back then was actually a shot of whiskey, and you can imagine how Mother felt about that. Just the thought of alcohol was enough to make her drunk with anger, yet she knew better than to argue with the doctor. She saved her energy for my father.

Every morning their work would commence with him dictating letters while she did the typing, and they'd squabble over the commas and periods. I now admire that attention to detail, but at the time I enjoyed the power bestowed upon me whenever my parents went out and left me in charge of the office; a nine-year-old, getting clients to sign documents and handing them their receipts. A *big shot*. True to form, I was treated like an adult, so finding fun things to do was largely my responsibility.

Our High Street apartment was a railroad flat, the rooms running in a straight line from the front to the back of the building with doors in between. In the first of these rooms was my parents' office; a rounded area that adjoined a square living room. This housed Daddy's huge wooden desk, a typewriting area where Mother sat off to the side and typed with arthritically bent hands, and some gray metal filing cabinets. All that appeared to be missing were bookshelves, but then, there were no books or magazines in our home. My folks were always busy socially—fishing and playing bridge—or taking care of the business. They didn't read. Never mind that I longed for books and magazines—I'd have to wait until I left home to fulfill my thirst for these. In the meantime, I explored an alternative source of information and escapism: the movies.

Sitting in the dark under that dusty funnel of light as it projected wondrous images onto a square white screen, I'd be transported into a magical world of make-believe romance, drama, and comedy: Janet Gaynor and Charlie Farrell in *Seventh Heaven*; Clara Bow and Buddy Rogers in *Wings*; Buster Keaton in *The General*. These were just some of the films that made an indelible impression on my youthful psyche.

During the twenties and thirties, there were five local theaters—the Sigma, Faraut, Regal, Rialto, and Schines Ohio—and while this might sound like a lot for a sleepy town, in those days there wasn't an old act that didn't play Lima. What's more, there evidently wasn't an old pervert who didn't pass up the opportunity to make a move on a small kid, because it was at the Rialto on Main Street that someone tried to molest me. One afternoon

I was there with my best friend, Hilda Whinemuller, and when she wanted to go home I decided to stay a little longer. That left me all alone. In an instant, some decrepit guy parked himself a couple of seats away, pulled out his shlong, and began jacking off while rubbing his foot against my ankle.

I knew nothing about sex and I had never seen a male organ, but I was inherently aware that this wasn't right. My parents had continually warned me, "Don't talk to strangers. Don't take candy. Don't let anybody try to lead you away," and I'd grown up absolutely terrified. I therefore raced home and told my mother what had happened, before we raced back to the theater and informed the manager. By then it was dinnertime, there were very few people around, and Mr. Choke-the-Chicken had slipped away. The manager said, "We know who these men are, but we can't do anything about them until they've been identified by a victim. So, the next time he comes in, I'll have him arrested and then give you a call." And that's precisely what happened: The next time that old bastard walked into the theater, they dragged him off to the police station, I identified him, and then after that I don't know what happened. He probably got off with a small fine. He should have been beheaded.

Still, nothing could put me off going to the movies. I *loved* them. Until I was ten they were all silents, but then in 1927 I saw the first talkie, The *Jazz Singer,* starring Al Jolson, and I was truly inspired. Like several early talkies, that film had silent passages with subtitles, and I remember seeing another such picture that featured a big fire scene with a lady sticking her head out of the window. At the bottom of the screen it said, "My fiancé!" but I read it as "My finance!" and thought, "Why is she yelling about her money at a time like this?" I swear I got straight A's at school.

Through junior high my best subjects were art, music, and writing, but I didn't do as well in math and I dropped out by the time we got to solid geometry. The teacher was a lesbian, but for some reason she was partial to boys, so I couldn't wait to get out of that class. I really excelled at the piano and I would play all the fancy things, even though I was always super-nervous when playing in front of people. The foot pedal shook, the whole room shook, but I could play better than any kid in Lima. I studied once a week with a variety of teachers who came to the house and who helped build my classical repertoire.

My other instrument was the saxophone, and again this was a case of Mother taking charge. When I was fourteen, she bought me a sax, as well as a gorgeous bracelet to go with it, after being impressed by an all-female band that she had seen. I guess this was her way of pushing me towards showbiz. Accordingly, every week for the next two years I was home-tutored by a boozy old guy who played clarinet in some local outfit. He always stank of liquor, but we'd sit in the living room with our metal music racks and play for an hour; him with his clarinet, me with my sax. What a sight. He had me play classical and I became pretty good, performing Donizetti's *Lucia di Lammermoor* in school assembly like a real hotshot. Not every kid can do that, but you see, I was already headed for a career onstage without any idea this was happening.

Women want men, careers, money, children, friends, luxury, comfort, independence, freedom, respect, love, and $3 panty hose that won't run.

Every year the seventh and eighth grades staged a show, and both times I had the second lead, which was the funny role. First I played a duchess in a conical hat, and the next year I portrayed Emelina Scroggs, a total yawn who never got the guy. Even back then the role fit me, although I stopped the show with my sweet, high singing voice. I wasn't cracking jokes, I was on the straight and narrow, but everyone saw something in me that I wasn't aware of. I could imitate every teacher's walk and mannerisms, and I'd bring the house down. I didn't think much about this, I just did it naturally, but other people said, "She's funny." I didn't know I was funny.

Initially, I pictured myself sitting in the spotlight at the concert grand. I didn't care about being center stage. I just wanted to be beautiful and sought-after and coddled, and my humor emerged partly because I was quick-witted and partly as an unconscious means of masking my insecurity. While being voted Best Girl Dancer and Most Talented Pupil, I attracted the attention of my peers mostly by playing the piano or by making what they considered to be comical observations about the world around us. As a result, I was always being asked to do a turn, and this was especially true in high school.

Central High and South High were mortal enemies, but Central had the rich kids, so again I stood out for all the wrong reasons. However, I can remember a little sorority party where I was the show, and suddenly I felt like I was *it*. At the time, there was this chant for the popular comic actor Eddie Cantor: "We want Can-tor, we want Can-tor . . ." Well, on another occasion I was at a school dance and on an upstairs level of the YMCA there was a piano. I was down on the main floor and the whole crowd was chanting, "We want Dri-ver, we want Dri-ver . . ." In other words, "Get up here." People would always put me at the piano, I'd make small asides, and that's how I began to develop an act. I'd talk a little, play like Victor Borge, and the first thing I knew, I was standing up and getting a laugh.

A lot of my comedy influences came via the radio. Made by the telephone company, our first one was installed inside our Electron Building apartment and looked like a shield that had been slapped on the wall. It could only pick up three stations, but these were enough for me to hear many of the era's most celebrated comic talents: Jim and Marian Jordan portraying the embattled married couple Fibber McGee and Molly; Freeman Gosden and Charles Correll as that hapless Harlem duo Amos 'n' Andy; and Fred Allen, Jack Benny, and Bob Hope, whose perfect timing and deadpan delivery I always admired. Naturally, I absorbed a lot of what these comedians did and automatically copied them, but I still never considered myself funny.

Throughout these years I always had a major crush on some boy, invariably one who was smart. Most girls went for the football and basketball stars, I went for the brains, even though looks were also important to me. Don't forget, I had a complex about my own looks, exacerbated by a lack of clothes, yet the knowledge that I was sharp meant that my hang-ups didn't hold me back when it came to the brightest boys; guys who I was crazy about and who would remain friends 'til death do us part. They weren't really boyfriends—I'd invite them to a dance or they'd invite me. Some of the girls dated steady and heavy, but I wasn't that type.

I hate smart sales clerks. I said to one, "What do you have in lingerie?" She said, "More than you'll ever have!" If it wasn't for my Adam's apple, I'd have no shape at all.

Once I was in ninth grade, I had access to guys from the better neighborhoods—*oh, baby.* Until then I'd never met one who interested me, but these were the hotshots of the town. And Miss Watson, who taught geometry, would always take an interest in my affairs. An elegant, delicate beauty who resembled Deborah Kerr, she could have passed for a movie star. Instead, she was an old maid who lived at the home of Hilda Whinemuller, just two blocks from our apartment, and I guess hearing about the ups and downs of my not-so-dangerous liaisons provided her with some light relief amid a staid existence.

Another of Central High's perpetual old maids was Miss Schwartz. She was smooth-fat as opposed to lumpy-fat—smooth, stretched-to-the-limit-fat—and she was the world's greatest grammar teacher. Because of her, we parsed and analyzed and emerged with a college education, and to this day I thank her for my understanding of the English language. Which is more than I can say for Miss Kellogg, a mean, heavy old bitch who sported purple bloomers and greasy hair in a bun. Like Miss Tullis, who'd made fun of my *Ben-Hur* perfume and fur-trimmed dress in the third grade, Miss Kellogg loved to humiliate me in front of the class. Some people make a living being cruel, and she really enjoyed it. Then there was Miss Howie, who attended our church and sang out of the corner of her mouth in a deep, almost masculine contralto voice. Fat and ugly as sin, she was built like a Hummer; a Hummer humming.

A few years earlier, following a disagreement with the Lutheran minister, my mother had told Daddy and me that we were transferring to the Methodist church, where we now sat in the same pew every Sunday. I have no idea what the difference was about, but I do know that, at both churches, Mother objected vociferously to baptisms involving immersion (which, in my eyes, always looked like the minister was trying to *drown* the kid). To her way of thinking, sprinkling water was the only acceptable method. Still, she was a valued contributor at our Methodist house of worship, where she devised an ingenious solution to the problem of small children growing impatient during a sermon: junior church. This was downstairs, where Sunday school usually took place, and it presented the adult service in a simplified form—brilliant.

Not that any of this ignited my theological aspirations. When I was a sophomore in Miss Hieronymous's class, I wrote a paper on the hereafter that she read to the students, and I'm sure she was astounded because I was already an atheist. From early childhood, whenever my great aunts and uncles died, I'd see them lying in the box and think, "Well, *she* ain't going nowhere." That opinion has never changed.

The Great Depression that had commenced in 1929, when I was twelve, hit hard during my high school years. Banks closed and few people had the money to spend on insurance, so my father's business virtually ground to a halt. Since the rent for our apartment was next to nothing, our lives weren't affected drastically, yet Daddy was worried and he spent two years with his head in his hands. He still oversaw the farm—buying livestock and rotating the crops—but he did so in a business suit. That man wasn't a farmer.

Lima didn't suffer like certain other parts of the country, but to me the place was boring and I couldn't wait to get out. So, when my mother arranged for me to attend Chicago's Sherwood Conservatory of Music immediately after graduating high school, I was overjoyed. Chicago, the big city, promised so much: clubs, concert halls, theaters, restaurants, major avenues of shops, and the opportunity to explore these and meet new boys without any old folks breathing down my neck. By now, Daddy was seventy-two, Mother was fifty-five, and I felt like an apprentice in a nursing home. However, the moment those two dear people put me on a train with nothing but a small suitcase I was scared out of my mind. For the first time, I truly was all alone. The journey to Chicago took five hours, and soot and smoke blew everywhere as that steam locomotive chugged along the tracks. It was like a scene out of an old movie.

In September 1934, Chicago was not only moving on from the era of Al Capone, but it was also starting to pick itself up from the ravages of the Depression. This had seen the city's employment cut in half, wages decline by 75 percent, downtown's

Lower Wacker Drive dubbed the "Hoover Hotel" by hundreds of destitute men who called it home, and many who did have jobs receiving their wages in the form of homemade money called scrip. Post-Prohibition, and about eighteen months into the presidency of Franklin D. Roosevelt, this metropolis on the banks of Lake Michigan, with its hectic thoroughfares and huge skyscrapers, was once again buzzing to its own rhythm, and for me it was fascinating and beautiful and scary.

At first, I stayed in the most awful, sparse, prisonlike room at a YWCA, with a fire escape outside my window. It scared the crap out of me, and so did the El (elevated) trains that I'd take in the wrong direction around the downtown Loop. I was so frightened of everything that I broke out in bold hives; huge swellings that were a sure sign I was in a state of panic. I knew I had to get away from my rotten living quarters.

The school where I studied piano, voice, harmony, and theory, was located in the Fine Arts Building on South Michigan Avenue, across from the Art Institute, and the registrar there found me au pair work and accommodation in a number of family homes furnished with a piano on which I could practice. Unfortunately, none of those situations worked out. One saw me being worked like Cinderella, so I was gone within days, and another had me living with mobsters in an absolutely gorgeous apartment. It was the classic gangster-and-moll setup, but they employed a maid and there wasn't anything for me to do. Still, that maid *hated my guts*. To her idiotic way of thinking, I was a threat, yet she didn't have to worry about me sticking around. It was absolutely sinister there.

Next, I was placed in the twelfth-floor home of that horny bastard Sam Loseff, where everything was going great until he put his greasy mitts all over me. At that point, while taking my parents' advice to avoid making a fuss over nearly being raped, I decided enough was enough. I stayed on until I found work as a cashier in the cafeteria of the Victor Lawson YMCA, located downtown on Chicago Avenue, and at last I was happy.

Now I could live in my own darling place just two blocks away; a huge room above Ye Olde Southern Tea Shoppe, run by an old lady who had spent her entire life in the theater (or, as she preferred to call it, "thee-a-tuh"), taking troupes on the road. She had bought the mansion of former Chicago Mayor Julian S. Rumsey, installed the Tea Shoppe on the ground floor, and rented the rooms above to some very creative people. Located on Huron Street, opposite the Episcopal Church, it was a wonderful place to live. And since the McKinlock Campus of Northwestern University was nearby, I also had access to these really bright guys who were studying to be doctors, dentists, and lawyers. Some of them made *wonderful* beaux.

My photographs don't do me justice. They look just like me. . . .
When I go to the beach, even the tide won't come in.

My main guy was like a cross between Franchot Tone and Fred Astaire, and I was nuts about him. Bright, skinny, and studying to be a doctor, he was named Wayne Field Cameron and I had an ankle bracelet with "WFC" engraved on it. When my mother asked what that stood for, I said, "Women's Friendship Circle."

She and my father would always surprise me with a visit, because Mother expected to turn up and discover that I was a prostitute living with some gangster. She should have been writing sex novels.

Wayne, meanwhile, decided to give me a blood test. I think he was trying to figure out whether or not to screw me, but he said it was an assignment and I bought it. You see, he and I had been dating for about a year, and we'd do heavy necking—heavy, heavy standup necking—in a private room at Ye Olde Southern Tea Shoppe. Well, sure enough, one night he tried to go all the way, but for some reason he just quit. I didn't know what was going on and he probably thought, "Oh, this kid is so dumb." Not long after, he gave up altogether.

My next relationship was with a cartoonist called Jeff Keate, who specialized in sports cartoons on which he'd work all night long. When I'd arrive for the breakfast shift at the Lawson building at six in the morning, he would be in a nearby office mailing out his night's work. That's how we got acquainted, and soon we began dating. Jeff's father was the editor of a big newspaper in the Northwest, and the family was very highbrow and well-to-do. So, when his mother came to town and saw me behind the cashier's counter in the cafeteria, she gave me a big black eye. After all, what the hell was her son doing with a cashier in the YMCA?

A short time later, when I returned from a visit to Lima, Jeff dropped me for a girl who he was probably screwing. We'd nevertheless remain lifelong friends, and he would end up marrying three times. The first wife reportedly met with his family's approval, but thereafter it was downhill all the way, and his last marriage was to a butch-looking pianist whom I met while we were both performing on the Dutch cruise ship *Prinsendam*. She was about six foot one and had the face of a bulldog. I've still got letters from Jeff in which he wrote, "Oh, if I had only married you when I was young . . ." He realized what a big help I would have been, especially with my interest in comedy.

When I first arrived at Sherwood I was not a vocal student, but one day I was messing around singing and someone heard me hit C above High C. That got me studying with Madame Arendt, a great beauty with long, dark hair pulled back in the style of a señorita, who was crazy about my voice. As a small kid back in Germany, she had sat on the knee of composer Johannes Brahms, and her musician father had been brought to this country by the Steinway Company. So, while she was nuts about me, I was pretty knocked out by her own credentials. She lived in the southwest suburb of La Grange and had me as a guest in her home several times. She even wanted me to marry her son, but there was no way. He was such a *schlub*.

As a piano student, I was very nervous. Shaky, shaky, shaky. I couldn't get past the first few bars of a number during evaluations. One of the examiners, Miss Keller, was an ugly old maid with stone-gray hair, and I'll never forget what she said: "Miss Driver looks so good at the piano, it's too bad she can't play." I just blew it. But I did look good.

As it happens, I was always fine at my recitals. Clearly there was something about the smell of the crowd, and that's how it's been my entire life. Performing comes naturally to me, but I've never had a good audition. Maybe I don't like the pressure of being judged. My roommate, Helen, who was also a vocal student, had to force people to attend her recitals, but mine were always standing-room only. You see, she didn't have it. *I* had it. In fact, even during my rehearsals everyone would gather by the door and peek in. I was born with the ability to attract attention, and I was largely aware of this, but I still felt insecure. I was never what I thought I ought to be, and, of course, I didn't like my looks. They undermined everything.

Most people get an appointment at a beauty parlor. I was committed. I spent seven hours there, and that was just for the estimate. The receptionist told me, "Lady, we do repairs, not reclamations." That ugly, insulting broad. She's had so many face-lifts, there's nothing left in her shoes!

I went to all these different jazz clubs, and I myself wanted to sing, so one time I auditioned. There was a large room and they put me at the far end, at which point I realized this was a joke. Obviously, they'd taken one look at me and thought, "Christ, what an ugly kid!" Still, as that Loseff guy knew, I did have big tits. And I also had some wonderful times with all those rich boys I was dating.

We'd go to the Edgewater Beach Hotel, a lavish, pink-stucco, Spanish-style resort on the lakefront, with its Beach Walk and Marine Dining Room, where on any given night we could enjoy top dance orchestras led by the likes of Roger Pryor, who was about to marry actress Ann Sothern. At the Blackhawk Restaurant on Wabash Avenue we'd watch bandleader Kay Kyser present his contest, the Kollege of Musical Knowledge. And there was also the College Inn restaurant inside the magnificent Hotel Sherman, where Isham Jones's all-white jazz orchestra was a major attraction on the local scene. Frequented by celebrities and members of high society, these were swell places that contributed to a fun nightlife, as did the little Near North Side dives where we'd catch jazz greats such as Art Tatum.

During this period I was also exposed to some of the era's most celebrated classical artists, including Russian composer Sergei Rachmaninoff performing with the Chicago Symphony Orchestra, and Norwegian soprano Kirsten Flagstad and Wagnerian tenor Lauritz Melchior appearing at the Civic Opera House in *Der Ring des Nibelungen* and *Tristan und Isolde*. All of this amounted to the most incredibly rich cultural life, yet after three years in Chicago, having concluded there was no future for *me* as an opera star or concert pianist, I knew it was time to leave.

My regular piano teacher, Georgia Kober, was president of Sherwood College, and while I was studying with her, she was invited to play on the gold piano at the White House. Then there was Madame Arendt, who had never made it big, big, big in our country, but who had sung opera in South America. These people were clearly gifted, I was not, and I certainly wasn't going to bang my head against a brick wall, so that's when I decided to go home and take a secretarial course. My mother, needless to say, would hear none of it. Don't forget, she was in charge.

She wasn't all that upset I was quitting Sherwood, but she also wasn't about to let me give up music, so at Mother's urging I obtained a scholarship at Bluffton College—a Mennonite liberal arts school located on sixty beautifully wooded acres about fifteen miles northeast of Lima. There I could study to become a public school music teacher . . . or so she thought. No way did I want to teach. And besides, the lecturers were so dumb. I mean, proposing to instruct first-graders on how to walk like an elephant? *Please*. Paying no attention whatsoever to the musical side of things, I concentrated with all my heart and soul on subjects such as literature, history, psychology, and philosophy, and the result was that I received a fine education. Nevertheless, I was always in trouble.

Founded in 1899 by regional leaders of the General Conference Mennonite Church, Bluffton College aimed to provide its students with a solid grounding in peace, love, religious faith, and clean living. So, when cigarette smoke was detected in my room, it was an immediate black mark. And I earned another after parading naked through the dormitory halls with only curlers, a belt, and a rose between my teeth. You can bet your life *that* woke everyone up. In truth, I wasn't a smoker or a streaker, but having come from the big city I thought I was hot shit— especially next to a bunch of creationist students who, like my mother, believed every word in the Bible was unarguable fact. To me, they were full of naive ideas, even though that's what the school was all about, and so I was highlighting the fact that I was different.

For three years I'd seen the greatest jazz musicians and finest symphony orchestras, and now here I was, in the country, among people who had experienced nothing but a simple farm life. Still,

I did hook up with some interesting kids at Bluffton, including Jean Fretz and Rebecca Mavety, who roomed next door to me and would remain lifelong friends; and Milburn Diller, who basically has a lot to answer for.

Six-two with eyes of blue, a brilliant mind, and movie-star good looks, Milburn was a hotshot at the school during my time there. Up until then, the Dillers had been *the* family in Bluffton, and as Milburn was dating Jean Fretz, he and I became very close friends. Jean was a pretty girl from a well-to-do family, and she was crazy about Milburn. He, meanwhile, wanted to double-date by setting me up with his older brother, and I initially resisted— I could play *so* hard to get—until I was invited to a party at the Diller home and first set eyes on Sherwood. Suddenly, I became a lot easier.

Boasting a terrific physique and the most beautiful blue eyes, Sherwood was my idea of terribly handsome; a big-city boy who was home from California to visit his mother. *Oh baby*, it was lust at first sight. I was twenty when we met, he was twenty-four, and I was immediately hooked. We'd go to Lima, dance to the jukebox, drink Cuba Libras (rum and Coke), and before long I lost my virginity. It was a matter of not being able to fight him off. And although my inexperience meant that I couldn't compare his performance to that of anyone else, I have to say I was disappointed—it was like the Peggy Lee song, "Is That All There Is?" My enjoyment apparently wasn't his concern. In time I'd be led to believe it wasn't my concern, either.

To hear Sherwood talk, he was going to rule the world and become the first trillionaire. What *talk!* What a *talker!* Clearly, he was bright, and he did have some incredible ideas. Yet, as I'd soon discover, he couldn't put the words into effect because his mind was already a total mess. None of this was evident when we started dating. But then, there was a lot that I didn't know. Sherry, as everyone called him, had dropped out from two colleges—first Bluffton, and then Miami University in Athens, Ohio—because he was convinced he knew more than any of the teachers in those "cesspools of education." Next, his mother, Maude, had bought him a roadster so that he could leave for the West Coast—maybe he had a job there for thirty minutes—but he'd then sold the car in order to have enough money to return home. As I'd learn, this is what he always did when he was out of cash. It should have been a warning sign that all of our dates were taking place with his mother's car and her money.

Ordinarily, the whole idea of getting a job was out of the question not just for Sherwood, but for all of the other family members who had grown accustomed to their role as small-town big shots. His father, Waldo, had founded Diller Manufacturing, which had subsequently merged with the Readrite Meter Company, a subsidiary of Triplett that specialized in radio equipment and based itself out of a building on Cherry Street in Bluffton, not far from the railroad tracks. When, in 1927, Waldo had committed suicide on those tracks by driving in front of a train, Maude had received the payout from a double-indemnity insurance policy, somewhat compensating her for the fact that her husband had been screwing her sister Jessie, knocked her up, and left her with a kid. It was a real-life soap opera.

Jessie had been married to a cellist and together they'd had a retarded child. When the kid was five, she had chloroformed it. Waldo and Maude had then gone to bat and seen her through the murder trial, using their money and their clout to ensure she avoided the rap by entering a convent and converting to Catholicism. However, after Jessie had subsequently emerged from the convent and moved into the family home, Waldo had dorked her and she'd gone to California to have his kid before returning and claiming she had adopted it. The fact that the boy looked like the double of Waldo was neither here nor there!

When Waldo died, the insurance money should have enabled Maude and her children, Sherwood, Milburn, and Jeane, to retain a pretty nice lifestyle, but they just spent it without investing a dime or doing a stroke of work. It didn't make sense. They never appeared to contemplate what would happen if none of them got a job. They just continued to walk around with their noses in the air, so I didn't have a clue as to what had gone on behind the scenes before I ever got involved with the Dillers. Only afterwards would I discover things little by little. I'd get to know old Aunt Jessie and her son, Pat, and seeing Waldo's photo made things as clear as the nose on my face.

In the meantime, almost as soon as Sherry and I slept together, I became pregnant. The word for that is fertile, or *fecund*, which makes the whole thing sound a lot more poetic. Since I'd been told that you shouldn't screw until you get married, I immediately dropped out of school—I couldn't be around those farm girls who already considered me to be a scarlet woman. In their eyes I would now be a *fecund slut*. And there was also no way I could tell my mother—she would have died on the spot.

So, Sherwood and I eloped to Covington, Kentucky, and I then used my artistic talent to change the date on the marriage license before handing it to Mother and announcing I was pregnant. Of course, her rheumatism flared up when she learned that we'd supposedly married several months earlier, but at least she believed I had still been a virgin.

On our wedding night Fang brought a book to bed. I wouldn't mind if he read. He colored! He is so cheap, my wedding ring turned my whole body green. And you wouldn't believe the engagement ring. He said it was a square-cut emerald. It was a Chiclet!

In those days, in that little town of 2,500 people, there was no other way. And I also didn't want my oldest child, Peter, growing up with the then-prevalent stigma of being illegitimate. This is a secret I've held on to all these years. Now, however, with both Peter and Mother long gone, I can tell the truth.

The only person who didn't blow apart when Sherwood and I divulged we were married was my dad—a precious man, a gentleman—although both he and Mother would have been happy for me to remain an old maid all my life. She was totally distraught at the idea of Sherry and me getting together, whereas Maude Diller had heart palpitations over the thought of someone else joining her precious family. Still, that's what happened.

Always ready for change, I threw myself headlong into the whole marriage and motherhood routine. We occupied one large bedroom in the Dillers' old Victorian house and I gave it a makeover, adorning it with flowers and painting it all white. (I was in my *white period*.) And I also did a lot of cooking. At the same time, I took the pregnancy very seriously, walking up and down the surrounding country roads with the Diller dog, a floppy old spaniel called Mr. Deeds.

On the surface, then, things were running pretty smoothly; yet it didn't take long for the neighbors to start telling me things. Nobody thought I should have married Sherry. *Nobody*. I was madly in love—he was so handsome—but they'd said, "Don't you *dare* marry him. Don't even *think* about marrying him." They had never explained why. It was just a case of "Don't." You see, he already had a reputation. The town knew him. I didn't.

From the minute I joined that family, it was obvious how strange they all were—never working, rarely socializing, and always peeping through windows instead of answering the front door. Now, learning some of their history made me realize the truth was even worse, but I was still full of youthful optimism. After all, spurred on by impending fatherhood, my husband was actually starting his own business.

As I was about to discover, few things involving Sherwood Diller ever turned out as planned.

Three

STEPPING IN
MANURE

Soon after Sherwood and I got married he rented part of a big old barn in Bluffton and set up the Diller Company, manufacturing and selling fluorescent lamps when fluorescents were still very new. In fact, he invented *indirect* fluorescent lighting—there wasn't anything like it—and it started to sell. The man undoubtedly had a high IQ, yet it didn't mean a thing. Your IQ has nothing to do with whether or not you're crazy.

His business had the potential to be very, very big . . . if it was run properly. All enterprises start small, but the first thing he did was put up a huge sign—THE DILLER COMPANY. He and his family were always thinking wrong. They were concerned about how things looked, not about what was happening, and their belief that they were better than anybody else undermined everything. When I realized that's how they felt, *oh my God*, it was an eye-opener.

For instance, when their minister came to wish Sherwood well with his new business, he wouldn't let him in. He didn't want the minister to see that he had only a small operation. Never mind that it was great, or that to help it succeed he had to get people on his side and let word of mouth do the rest. He wouldn't let the minister in! How about *that* word of mouth? Again, it was all about what the neighbors would think—all for show.

Sherwood and his brother, Milburn, were in this business together, and the brother was even more useless. He was lazy. Lazy and too good to work. They'd be packing the goods to put them on the train and Milburn would be reading the packing paper. He also wouldn't get up until noon or make any calls. I asked Mrs. Diller, "Shouldn't Milburn be making these calls in the morning?" but she didn't want to know. She'd always defend him. In fact, when I'd point out how he was sitting around, reading novels, she'd look at me knowingly and say, "They are a good way to learn about life." My opinion was that he'd learn way faster if actually he did some work.

Whenever I spoke about the boys and their business, Maude would refute my ideas in a very condescending way. "We've been in the *mannafacturing* business for years," she would say, trying to put me in my place. I'd be tempted to correct her, "The word is *manufacturing*," but I never confront anybody, anywhere, anytime. I may cut them off, but I don't confront. (I may have to *kill*, but I don't confront.) Real quick I realized that I'd stepped in manure. Friends of mine would come to visit from Lima, and the Diller boys would look out through the blinds and refuse to let them in. Helen, my former Sherwood college roommate, also came by—imagine this—and again they wouldn't let her in. I had to go outside and talk to her in the car. What was I supposed to say? It was like living with the Addams Family. Still, after Peter, our first child, was born in September 1940, I had little choice but to take care of him in that madhouse, so I just put up and shut up.

Thankfully, the Dillers' snooty, snobby attitude no longer extended towards me. I was now embraced with open arms, and Sherwood's sister, Jeane, treated me like a new sibling. She had a Ph.D. in osteopathy, yet throughout her life she'd never make more than $2,000 a year. Like the rest of them, she didn't work. She always had an office, but she never gave an appointment. Many years later, on my way home from a job, I was about to drive past her office when I decided to drop in and say hello. So, I parked the car, walked to the office, which was then in the back of a large drugstore, and when I knocked on the door I could hear someone in there. She, however, wouldn't answer. Next I went to the payphone and called, but she wouldn't answer the phone, so I finally got back in the car and drove home. *Craziness.* I didn't take it personally, because she didn't know who was calling, but how could she make a living that way?

Dr. Jeane was very close to her mother; so close that the

mother kept her from ever getting married. At one time she was engaged, but then Maude had a little talk with Jeane and convinced her that, having attained a degree in osteopathy, she should dedicate herself to her profession. The guy she was supposed to marry had a lucky escape. And she never used that degree, anyway.

Meanwhile, despite all its potential and Sherwood's best efforts, the Diller Company didn't last long. How could it, when the guys in charge were avoiding their customers? That whole family was nuts. *Nuts*. And it was also headed towards a serious reality check. One day I ordered some groceries and got an inkling that all was not well in terms of money when the store demanded cash up front. Maude soon wouldn't be able to hold back the truth—or avoid facing it—any longer: She was broke, and that would mean selling the house and moving out of town. After all, there was no way she and her kids could stay where they had been looking down their noses at people. They would remain snooty and snobby all the way to the poorhouse.

On Sunday, December 7, 1941, at around one o'clock in the afternoon, I was in the living room, listening to a symphony performance on the radio, when an announcer broke in with the news that Pearl Harbor had been bombed. Like most people, I was shocked and stunned, but for Sherwood the Japanese attack resulted in some work. A few months later, he landed a job at the U.S. Government's Willow Run bomber plant in Ypsilanti, Michigan, just outside of Detroit, where B-24s were being manufactured as part of the new war effort. By the following year, this mile-long facility—then the biggest of its kind anywhere in the world—would hire more than 42,000 men and women who'd combine to produce one four-engine Liberator every hour, each containing 100,000 parts.

Sherry went there ahead of me while I sorted out the items that he and Milburn had left in the vacated barn of their aborted fluorescent-lighting venture: ladders and brooms, as well as lamps that were still in stock. I made a single trip to nearby Findlay and recouped some money by selling everything in one day. That was the only time Maude let me drive her car. So ended the expansive but short-lived dreams of the Diller Company.

Shortly afterwards, Peter and I followed Sherry to Ypsilanti, where, over the course of three years at Willow Run, he rose from the very bottom, earning 95¢ an hour, to making $1.60 as an inspector, working nine-hour days, six days a week. He learned to inspect the hydraulics, the electrics, the structure, everything on an airplane. As I've said, he was not dumb, and this job, together with the fact that he had a child, also stopped him from getting drafted. (Not that he would have passed the eye test—vanity precluded him from wearing glasses.)

At work the signs were encouraging. At home, in our attic apartment on Oakwood Avenue, it was a different story. There my husband wouldn't do a *thing*. Not only did I paint the entire place, paint the furniture, and take care of whatever odd jobs needed doing, but if, for example, I needed some ice, I'd have to be the one to take a wagon and get it. He would just plain refuse. In fact, the furniture that I painted never had door knobs. I didn't know how to fit them and he wasn't about to do it, so we had to claw everything open. It didn't make sense, but then, nothing did.

Fang loves crowds. It's not that he's gregarious—he's a pick-pocket. . . . He once tried to run out on me, but the police arrested him for leaving the scene of an accident. . . . The other night he was reading the obituaries and he said, "Isn't it amazing how people die in alphabetical order?"

Regardless of my situation, I always managed to find something to enrich the soul, and while we were in Ypsilanti this turned out to be a beautiful Presbyterian church where I sang solos. One Sunday I had a fabulous aria and I wanted little Peter to hear his mommy sing, so Sherwood brought him to the service. It would be quite an event for a small kid to see his mother on the stage of this huge church, actually getting a little respect. However, just as I was about to sing, I watched Sherwood get up, grab hold of Peter, and leave. My heart was broken.

Talk about passive aggression—how to get to the core of a woman and destroy her. He was a mean jerk, yet I never made a scene; never throughout the course of our marriage. You dance around a sicko like that, because if you argue, you're the one who goes straight into the toilet, not him. And I also had no idea as to what I could do except try to make the relationship work. So, there we were, living in a home with a bed that consisted of a mattress on blocks, and I was making the most of everything; making it pretty and cooking great meals.

All I ever wanted at that point was to be a housewife, and eventually I'd end up with five kids, all the responsibility, and no way out. Still, I have to admit that I did want Sherwood's children, and there were, in fact, six of them, but we lost the second shortly after he was born. It was a breech birth, a blue baby who lived just two weeks in an incubator. He was named Perry, after my father. (Our youngest child would subsequently take that name.) Of course, I was devastated by the loss, but subconsciously I knew it was a blessing because he had a deformity of the hands and was possibly also blind. I immediately asked the doctor, "How long is it before I can have another baby?" That's how I thought: You got married and had children. On the other hand, what I tried to avoid thinking about was the process that caused me to have those kids.

We have far too many kids. At one time in the playpen there was standing-room only. It looked like a bus stop for midgets. It used to get so damp in there, we'd have a rainbow above it.

Sherwood was *lousy* at sex, the *world's worst*, just pumping away with absolutely no idea how to come. I felt like a trampoline. He'd want to jump on me all the time, and there were occasions when he'd get his way and a few hours later, I would deliver a baby. You're not supposed to do that. Once, when I was leaving for the hospital to give birth, he refused to accompany me. He was going to put me in a cab, but then a neighbor made him go. Because of his behavior, I can't think of him fondly. He was cruel. Cruel and brutal.

Our daughter Sally was born in November 1944, and right

from the start I suspected something wasn't quite right. Whereas a baby can usually sit on your lap and hold on to your neck, I'd have to grip her constantly or else she'd just flop and fall. That was the first clue. Another was her terrible projectile vomiting—a column of milk would shoot straight over my shoulder. I wasn't yet aware that she actually had a serious mental condition. That would come later when more was expected of her. And besides, none of this appeared to worry her father, who clearly had far more pressing concerns.

Sherry would come home from his blue-collar job in Willow Run, put on his suit and hat, get *The New York Times*, go down the road to a little coffee shop, and sit there, smoke, and drink coffee while reading the paper. Again, he was just putting on a show, in this case for the waitress and whoever else happened to be around. He wanted to look like a big shot. I mean, after a day's work, wouldn't you think he'd want to come home and relax? Oh no, let's go do the act. The worst was one time when both Peter and Sally were throwing up, Peter with colic and Sally with the whooping cough. I called the café, and Sherry wouldn't even come to the phone. Things like that just drove me insane.

The three years at Willow Run were easily his longest stretch of employment to date. Yet, ever since his time in California, he had loved it and wanted to live there. So, in 1945, when it became clear that the war was winding down and that the bomber plant would soon be closing, Sherry gained a transfer to the Naval Air Station in Alameda, a pristine, beautifully manicured little island that lies adjacent to Oakland, across the bay from San Francisco. This was a smart move on his part—he drove there in a car that was full of our belongings while Peter, Sally, and I traveled by train. But then, just a few days after our arrival, my dear spouse was out of a job.

I didn't know if he quit or if he was fired, and nobody ever told me the full reason. *He* certainly wouldn't tell me. All I heard was that there had been a dispute over a cup of coffee. He ended up going through another seventeen jobs within one year, and still I never discovered why. His attitude, the conviction that he knew better than anyone else, was enough to get him fired. All I knew was that he'd always wait until the money was gone and then sell the car that my parents had bought us.

Some jobs lasted a week, others lasted two. One was at a foundry, another was demonstrating toys in a schoolyard during recess, a third was as a night watchman—from which he got fired after falling asleep—a fourth was as a drill press operator . . . Sherry even had cards printed to say that he was in real estate, and he did pass the real-estate exam, but he never sold a thing. Then he was a taxi driver, and that actually lasted a year because, you see, it was an environment where he was in charge with nobody watching over him. He couldn't work under anyone. I remember him coming home from the drill press job and telling me that he'd been producing so much, they had to let him go. Yeah, *right*.

Fang is a good loser. He lost eleven jobs in one year. I can tell he isn't frightened of work by the way he fights it. He's been under a lot of pressure lately, though—three quilts and a blanket. When he wants breakfast in bed, I call AA and they talk him out of it.

I was living through all this, and doing so in a horrible Alameda housing project that had to be the ugliest place in the world. Located on the enticingly named Stalker Way, our building contained eight tiny two-bedroom units where everything was made of wood. Even the sink and shower were made of wood—remember, there was a shortage of metal during the war—while the kitchen had a kerosene stove. Of course, I was the one who had to get the kerosene, and as we were habitually between cars, I'd transport it in the baby buggy. It was, in short, the worst period of my entire life.

In March 1946, I gave birth to our third child, Suzanne, and returned home with her when she was just six hours old. Sherwood hadn't even called the hospital to ask how I was doing. Nevertheless, when he wasn't jumping on me, I did find time to do a few other things. I was very active as the music director at the First Presbyterian Church on Santa Clara Avenue, where I again sang in the choir. The organist, Howard Brubeck (Dave Brubeck's brother), taught music at Mills College in the East Bay area—he'd studied there under the famous French composer Darius Milhaud—so being in that big church was my idea of heaven. It didn't matter that I was an atheist. This was my other life, my escape, among people with whom I wanted to socialize.

That December, I conceived and wrote the most beautiful Christmas Eve presentation, including a recitative performed by soloists in between traditional Christmas carols. Brubeck was at the organ, a string quartet was over to one side, lit candles were everywhere, and a children's choir was way up in the balcony. Innovative as always, I had the kids sing through Campbell's Soup cans which totally changed the sound of their voices, and the overall effect was magnificent. I was so proud of that. Afterwards, having witnessed what I could do, a number of ladies at the church fingered me for shows, and I remember one particular occasion when they wanted a program about mothers. I wrote and performed an entire comic routine and it went down really well. Humor came naturally to me.

An old Jewish guy went into a confessional at a Catholic church and told the Father, "I'm a married man and yesterday I had sex with a twenty-year-old girl, twice." The priest said, "Well, why are you telling me? You're a Jew." The old guy said, "I'm telling everybody."

Another time, my voice succumbed to laryngitis in the middle of a show, so that darling Howard Brubeck took over by playing piano. I often felt close to death—under such pressure, living with hate—and those shows were my savior. Well, before long I had figured out a little routine. One Thanksgiving night I was asked to perform at the Alameda Naval Air Station, where I sang several different numbers, including both parts of Jeanette Mac-Donald and Nelson Eddy's "Indian Love Call"—"When I'm calling you-oo-oo-oo, oo-oo-oo . . ."—while interspersing everything with comedy. The show was a success, the organizers loved it, and my payment was a live turkey. They obviously thought I was a star in the making.

Can you picture me walking home with that thing in the early hours of the morning? It was *huge*. It must have weighed about thirty pounds, and there I was, pulling it by a string attached to its neck. Along the way I tried to make friends with it, but damn, that turkey had a nasty disposition, so when I arrived home I tied it to the outside of our front door (which is what one does in that kind of situation) and went to bed, and a short time later the doorbell rang. It wasn't the turkey. A couple who lived in our block had seen this poor, confused creature trotting like a maniac all over the play area, and immediately they thought, "It must belong to Diller!" Doesn't that say something? They told me, "We're farm people, so we'll kill it and share it with you." And that's what they did, taking half of my pay.

Back in Lima, my eighty-five-year-old father was starting to fade. His angina was giving him a lot of pain, and he in turn was giving my mother a fair amount of grief. As an adult I'd never had much of a relationship with him—he was an old, old guy. Yet, sensing that the end was near, I did want to articulate how I felt about him while he was still around, rather than dole out the praise after he was gone.

Dear Dad:

They tell me that sometimes you feel you're hearing, or rather, "list'ing to your last jaybird and seeing the woodbine twine for the last time." If there is any truth in this, I wish to express to you my gratitude for all you've given me during the thirty years of my happy life. I have you and Mother to thank for bequeathing me a healthy, strong, and durable body, a sound and resourceful mind. I must thank you, also, for an unusual childhood filled with useful and interesting experiences, for a fine education, and for love and help and understanding whenever I needed it.

You may rest assured you'll be admitted at the pearly gates after a long and successful life. If you think of it, you might put in a good word for me with St. Peter.

Love,

Phyllis

Some time later, when going through my parents' possessions after they had both passed on, I'd find this letter and, seeing its worn condition, realize how much it had been treasured and appreciated.

A few years earlier, while living at the Diller family home, I had befriended a New York gal named Eloise Travis, an Ali McGraw lookalike who had married a doctor in Bluffton. Older than me and very beautiful, she had always wanted to marry a country doctor, and since the Dillers would only associate with doctors and lawyers, it was natural that I ran into her. Thereafter we became lifelong bosom buddies, meeting and corresponding with one another on a fairly regular basis.

July 27, 1948

Dearest Eloise:

Today Sherry turned 35 and it is just 53 days till our blessed event. Peter is spending the summer in Los Angeles with Aunt Jessie & Pat, but the St. Louis Dillers don't know it (having forbid me to have anything to do with the L.A. relatives). I took him down myself and find them both

charming people. You had better not repeat this to a *soul* in
Bluffton, as it would be a particularly bitter pill coming from
any source there. However, I must say, they bring all this sort
of double dealing on themselves—I feel I should be left to
choose my own friends and make my own decisions . . .

It is late and I am terrifically weary—I feel like poor At-
las holding up the world, only I've got it in me!

Love—as ever
Phyllis

P.S. When you're in Lima, drop in and see Mother. My
father is giving her an *awful* time—senility combined with
a native cussedness.

A couple of months after I wrote that letter, Daddy died at the
age of eighty-six. On October 9, I gave birth to Stephanie, and
then about nine days later, we finally left our wooden hellhole
and moved into a home that my mother had bought us on San
Jose Avenue in Alameda. Basically, she had closed up everything
in Lima and come to California to save my life. The place that
she purchased was one of those old, old Victorian houses that
rises up into the sky. Located close to the water, it was divided
into five units, enabling us to rent out four of them and live in
the downstairs one. Mother knew what she was doing. Now I
could pay the bills and still have quite a lot of cash left over.

She and my father never had a clue as to how bad things were,
but it was obvious that Sherwood rarely earned a dime. The two
of them had always worked very hard, scrounging and scraping,

and now that Mother had my inheritance to pass along, she wanted me to divorce Sherwood. That's why she came to California; to get rid of him. And she was also there to organize things in her own unique way.

Little Stephanie was as bald as a billiard ball and my mother *adored* that newborn baby, sitting and rocking her for hours. However, she didn't like Sally—she sensed that she wasn't right in the head, and this would turn out to be true. What's more, it had been her idea to have Peter stay in Los Angeles with good old Aunt Jessie, who was a former teacher and a martinet when it came to raising children. It was all about Mother's gut feeling, as well as her conviction that I had too many children in not enough space. I wasn't overjoyed by this, but I went along with what she said because I was young, dumb, and needed help. And she was also giving me all this money, so I wasn't about to bite the hand that was feeding me. She was in a power position and we both knew it.

During this period, Mother and I had the grandest time ever. It was buddy time. She bought a green Nash LaFayette sedan and I'd drive while she was in the backseat, doing our errands and having a ball. Sherwood was working at Dodge Automotive, but then the factory went on strike, again he was unemployed, and there was some kind of confrontation between him and my mother. I'm not sure what went down, but I'll never forget returning home in the green LaFayette and seeing Sherry standing on the front porch, brooming. That was pretty unusual. He normally didn't do *anything*. Clearly, whatever Mother said had spurred him into "action"—which is more than I could ever do—but notice that he also chose to get busy where the whole world could see him.

Housework can't kill you, but why take a chance? The TV screen in our home is so filthy, for years the kids thought they were listening to the radio.

All the while, Mother was bending my ear, telling me I must get a divorce. I knew I was in trouble, but I told her, "I can't make that decision all by myself." Instead, I sought the opinion of my dear friend Reverend Glass, the minister at the Presbyterian church where I was music director. I called him, he came over to the house, and we had a very civil conversation:

"Does he beat you?"

"No."

"Is he a good father?"

"Yes."

"Does he fool around?"

"No."

"Then you have no problems and no grounds for divorce."

Thanks in part to these incredible words of wisdom, insight, empathy, and understanding—*please*—I stood by my apparently model husband. However, I also think that, subconsciously, a better voice told me to hold on. I instinctively knew the timing was off. I just used the opinion of Reverend Glass, whom my mother respected, to convince her that I couldn't leave Sherwood, and from that moment, I watched her fade away. Her work was done and her efforts hadn't succeeded. But if she only knew what a wonderful ending my story would have—what I do and what I've achieved—she would be so proud. After all, look how things ended up because I allowed them to play out in a slower way. It would eventually be Sherwood's idea that I should become a comic, and I never would have thought of that. Timing is everything. Something inside me has a kind of homing instinct.

Mother was only sixty-eight when she died in March 1949, six months after Daddy. She had never been a robust person, and the state of her health had always been psychosomatic, so the realization that I wouldn't divorce was enough to kill her. She had a stroke and that was that. However, there had been no breakdown in our relationship. She and I had the best time together. Of course, I felt lonely when she was gone, but it was also probably some kind of relief. Can you imagine living between two people who hate each other? As the pivotal person, I had to get along with everybody.

My inheritance included the fifty-five-acre P. M. Driver National Highway Farm in Beaverdam, Ohio, and $30,000 cash, so our money worries should have been over; but, of course, Sherwood couldn't wait to move to a better neighborhood. I don't care what you give people like him, they're going to be broke within a week. And people like me are dumb enough to do whatever it takes to make people like him happy. Then again, I wasn't exactly against the move.

With four rental units in our house, I was in charge of all those tenants, and that wasn't easy. I was a *stupid* landlady. For instance, I'd decorated the top apartment and a guy had moved in, but it was two weeks before I noticed that he had left without paying the rent. At the same time, there was this gossipy old Irish couple who bugged the hell out of me. They were always pointing their fingers at someone and saying something mean. So, I couldn't wait to get away from all that. I was not cut out to live with a house full of assholes. One was enough.

The result was that we picked up roots yet again and paid $17,500 cash for a sweet little split-level house at 1841 Fremont Drive in Fernside, the Beverly Hills of Alameda. Once there, I purchased some lovely furniture and I also bought Sherry a hot new Ford station wagon—the last one to have real wood. It was a beauty. My line of thinking—a totally warped line, but a line nonetheless—was that if he could drive around and act important, he'd somehow make a living. Well, blow *that* dream.

Instead of getting an ordinary job like everyone else, my husband was always working on some product that he envisioned earning him trillions. One was a basic, old-fashioned radio for children—why? *Why?* Another was a kids' sundial. And for *years* he worked on an airlift that would enable an airplane to pull several gliders like a train in the sky. He would spend hours smoking and drinking coffee while working on these harebrained schemes, and he'd do so in front of me and the kids. Meanwhile, every one of those kids' birth certificates listed their father's career as "Publisher." For posterity, like the present, he had to be a big shot.

We used to drive into the forest and take picnics with the kids, and one day while they were running around, Sherwood and I talked. I suggested therapy to him, and for a microsecond he let down his defenses and opened up just enough to almost agree to this. It was as if a ray of light shone in, but then he immediately clamped shut again and that was the end of it. It would have been like a crazy person admitting he's nuts. In his case it was never going to happen. He had become comfortable with a way of life in which he had absolutely no responsibility.

Due to our recent housing transactions, we got very thick with the realty agent, Mrs. Pillars, and she gave Sherwood a job soliciting business on the telephone in her office. Now, *that* he could do. He didn't have to face people. So, he stayed there for a while, until Pillars realized that he wouldn't go out to show the properties, and then shortly afterwards he got his best job ever, selling freezers and refrigerators at Sears, Roebuck & Co. This was when freezers were first introduced onto the market, so a blind idiot could have sold them. They came with a side of lamb or a side of beef—it was quite a deal. At least it helped him to stay there for three whole years.

Peter had rejoined us as soon as we'd moved to Fremont Drive, and Perry, our fifth child, was born in February 1950. Having been an only child myself, I thought it would be awfully good fun for the kids to have brothers and sisters, and I really enjoyed being with them. I loved feeding them and creating artwork with them and reading to them and teaching them to sing. And Peter was also displaying his own musical prowess—having found a banjo in a friend's basement, he'd been able to take it apart, put it back together, and learn how to play it to the point where I took him to a teacher and the teacher said, "I can't teach him any more." That's not a dumb kid. It was wonderful to see him and his siblings developing day by day. However, Sherry's earnings just weren't enough to take care of us, and before long my

$30,000 inheritance was gone, the Beaverdam farm had been sold for $5,000, and we were at the end. That's when I knew I had to get a job.

Always be nice to your children because they are the ones who will choose your rest home.

First off, I applied for some work at an apricot cannery and I turned up there in this chic suit, but they took one look at me and said I was over-qualified. I wonder why. Then I applied for a waitressing job and didn't get hired, so I started to think, "What can I do?" I knew that I could do housework—after a fashion— and I also considered myself to be a writer. I'd already tried to get an article published when we were living in that horrible wooden housing project, and a magazine had taken a look and sent me what I now realize was a fairly encouraging letter, advising me to refine the piece and resubmit it. I, however, had assumed this was just a plain old rejection.

The article basically provided a near-perfect description of where I now live in Brentwood; my dream house, although I had never seen it back then, of course. It had a room for painting, a room for music, a room with books—remember, I'd never had a room of my own—as well as a beautiful kitchen, and I went on and on and on before explaining that I would support all this with a printing press in the basement, printing money. That was a joke, but the intent was clear—I had tried to write my way out of the abyss, and I would continue to do so.

In the face of continual frustration and disappointment, I

didn't allow for much anger. I was always trying to become a better person, trying to get along with everybody, yet I do remember one occasion on Fremont Drive when a terrible rage got the better of me. I was alone in the living room, looking at my college scrapbook from the Sherwood Conservatory of Music, and suddenly I felt so overwhelmed by my situation that I threw the scrapbook into the fireplace and burned the damned thing. That was a gesture. No one knew about it, just me, and I never told anybody. It was too painful. It was a loss of hope. You know, "Forget it." Forget being smart, forget having any talent, forget dreaming about making something of myself. That was sad.

Now, however, I was slowly clawing my way back, trying to put myself in the mix, trying to step out and step up. Leafing through a local paper, I saw an ad: "Copy boy wanted at the *San Francisco Chronicle*." So, I put on my little hat and dress and went in person to apply for the job, only for a man to very gently tell me that it was intended for a young fella who'd start at the bottom; a kid who couldn't afford college fees to train as a journalist.

"It wouldn't be suitable for you," he explained, "but there is a small newspaper in San Leandro that is switching from a weekly to a daily. It would be a good idea for you to apply there."

He could say *that* again. Just a few doors from our house on Fremont Drive lived Abe Kofman, the guy who owned the *Alameda Times-Star* and the *San Leandro News-Observer*. He had often seen me while walking past our place, a young housewife with all these little kids. So, when I mentioned that I was interested in a writing job, Abe told the *News-Observer* editor to give me an audition—over the course of one week, I was to write an

entire Christmas issue. Well, that's what I did, and I was immediately hired at $75 a week, out of which I paid a maid named
Mabel Bridgewater $25 to babysit our children.

Mabel was a skinny little African-American lady with a wonderful sense of humor and a great laugh, and thanks to her help
around the home I was able to work and enjoy the company of
adults. I found this mentally stimulating. There now was a whole
world for me to explore: *my* world. I loved being a mother and
taking care of the creative end of homemaking—teaching the
children, taking them to the beach, cooking for them, and feeding them—but I wasn't cut out to do housework such as cleaning. I didn't like cleaning and I never really learned how to do
it well. I took the drapes down one time but forgot to remove
the little clips and they ruined the Bendix. They also ruined
the drapes.

April 13, 1951

Dearest Eloise:

I might as well be a nun in a convent, the life I lead. No
more of this social rat racing for me! Boy, is it frustrating. I
go NO PLACE except to the beach every Sunday . . . I go
to no teas, I belong to not one single organization . . . Oh
GOD what a wonderful ivory tower, and is it ever peaceful
up here! Nobody comes to call on me and I go to call on
nobody . . . nobody has us to dinner and we don't have anybody to dinner. A few very rare exceptions, maybe.

It is probably very difficult for you to picture me thus,
and I certainly couldn't get by with it in Bluffton, but what

a peaceful existence, just enjoying all these pretty children, reading, writing, Sherry and I spending all our free time together. He belongs to nothing, also. Goes no place. How about that?

Love,

Phyllis

Located just south of Alameda, San Leandro was a picturesque little city, with its own marina, older-style housing on tree-lined streets, an annual Cherry Festival, and a rapidly expanding population. As women's editor at the *News-Observer,* I penned a society column that referred to who and what I saw at a number of local parties, as well as a shopping column focusing on products that the storekeepers paid to have mentioned. That meant I didn't spend much time in the office. It was spent talking to advertisers and going around town, and every now and then I'd also be given a proper reporting assignment. I didn't know how to type until I got that job—I was self-taught—but before long my columns were attracting attention around the Bay Area, and, in the process, I was unwittingly honing skills that would later prove invaluable to me as a professional comedy writer.

You see, practically everything I wrote was injected with my own brand of humor, and judging by the feedback, the readers and advertisers clearly loved it. However, there was also a red-headed editor at the paper who hated my guts. His name was Ed Purcell, and he'd go out of his way to haze me. He was a boozer, and he would come in with these terrible hangovers and pick on people, including the little girl who was our society editor. Her typewriter rusted because he made her cry so much. He made me cry, too, but I'd never cry in front of him. I would go a block down to the Esso station and cry in the john.

Purcell was a freckle-faced monster and he was out to get me. Knowing how much I needed the money, he tried to fix it so that I would have just two days of work. He got it to the point where I was only handling the movie schedules, and that's not writing— so three months after joining, I had to quit. I needed to work five days a week and he just killed me, but here's the denouement: Years later he would come to one of my shows in Las Vegas and say that he wanted to write my book. Can you believe it? That asshole had some nerve.

And I had the last laugh.

Four

BELIEVING

You are the product of your own thought. What you believe
yourself to be, you are.

—CLAUDE M. BRISTOL, *The Magic of Believing*

In June 1951, after leaving the *San Leandro News-Observer*
and then failing to get a job as a music librarian at the *Oakland Tribune*, I found employment in the advertising office of
a large Oakland department store named Kahn's. A downtown
landmark consisting of a grand rotunda covered by a glass dome,
the building was four stories high, with the ad office and furniture on the top floor; housewares and bedding on the floor below
that; ladies' fashion apparel on the second level; menswear, books,
and jewelry on the main floor; and sale items in the basement.

A hotshot guy ran the ad office, while the assistant advertising
manager was a handsome gay man named Bill Shang. Then

there was a cute little girl artist, Jenny Day, and a young, pudgy, old-maid type who handled all of the basement goods and always had her nose stuck in the *Reader's Digest*.

Finally, there was the fashion editor who was totally full of herself—a snooty, bigheaded bitch who thought that her stool didn't smell. You see, my dear, she was in *fashion* and therefore above it all . . . at least, to her way of thinking. In truth, the only thing she was above was that bedding on the third floor.

For $75 a week I was put in charge of the newspaper and radio ad copy pertaining to the rest of the store. It was a heavy load, but I soon made a name for myself with my writing and my layouts. I worked closely with the printers concerning typeface and I made it an art. I'd use a lot of white space, which in those days many people thought was wasted space, but it was eye-catching and the buyers would call me to praise my work. I've always done things in my own special way. If you do that, you're going to get noticed. When the other girls in that office finished their work, they'd do their nails and read a novel. I, on the other hand, would go to the front desk, look at the figures, and study the loss leaders to see what items did best. That meant I was learning something, and I could also apply it to my job because I was turning out an awful lot of copy.

"Prices on our damaged refrigerators have been slashed. If demand is heavy, we can damage a few more."

I could outthink anybody when it came to ads and layouts. I was *hot* for advertising, and I got a great deal of pleasure out of knowing that. Of course, I lacked confidence because of my looks and because of the way that Sherwood treated me, but the work was slowly restoring my sense of self, and then something else came along to change my life completely.

On one occasion, just a couple of months after joining Kahn's, I had to deal with a buyer who was taking a full-page ad featuring prices listed from top to bottom for things like mattresses, pillows, and linens. She had to check this in minute detail because if, for example, a mattress was accidentally listed for 25¢, the deal would have to be honored. I therefore knew that I was going to be in her little cubbyhole-office for a long time while she went over all the details, and as she had a number of books in there I just reached up to the shelf and took one called *The Magic of Believing*. In those days I never wasted a minute. I was gung-ho, and as soon as I started reading that book I thought, "Jesus, this is talking to *me*."

I asked the woman if I could borrow the book and I took it up to my office, but as I continued to read it I wanted to underline things. Well, I wouldn't underline somebody else's book, so I called down to the bookstore, bought my own copy, and for the next two years *The Magic of Believing* became a system of thought for me as well as a way of life. Written by a lawyer, lecturer, investment banker, and foreign correspondent named Claude M. Bristol, this incredible tome described motivational techniques that make use of the subconscious mind, powers of suggestion, imagination, and self-belief to overcome everyday obstacles and achieve personal happiness along with professional success.

Thought is the original source of all wealth, all success, all material gain, all great discoveries and inventions, and of all achievement. . . . By using the dynamic force of believing, you can set all your inner forces in motion, and they in turn will help you to reach your goal.

—Claude M. Bristol

These were the kinds of words that transported me out of the fire into which I'd thrown my scrapbook of dreams and aspirations. Almost like a mantra, I'd keep re-reading the parts that I underlined—I didn't bother with the filler—and from here on it was straight up, all the way. I had a whole different slant. I *believed* that everything was going to work out, so even the setbacks that I'd experience wouldn't matter. Everything I'd touch would turn to gold.

Beforehand, I would run and hide and pull the covers over my head whenever anybody gave me a dirty look. If people said and did nasty things to me, I would accept them. I was so easily destroyed. However, after immersing myself in *The Magic of Believing* I accepted nothing negative. In fact, I imagined a protective device for myself: it was a white feather cape that wrapped around me, ensuring that, like water off a duck's back, nothing could ever get through. My hatred of confrontation meant that I didn't answer anybody back, but I developed a shield against all of the negative vibes that some people kept putting out.

If I did draw attention towards myself it was never intentional, and even though I had a wild laugh, I certainly wasn't an extrovert or the least bit pushy. I've always been one of the guys and I love comedy, so I invariably had plenty of laughs with them and maybe some people resented that. Then again, several of my coworkers became lifelong dearest buddies. These included the poet Rod McKuen, who had his own ninety-minute prime-time Saturday night show at KROW, the local radio station where I worked as a copywriter, publicist, and continuity girl after I was hired away from Kahn's in January 1952. And there was also KROW's female star, Wanda Ramey, who would soon be the first ever woman to host a daytime TV news show. Wanda was a beautiful Gene Tierney lookalike with a soft voice and a kind, generous nature, and she and I became bosom buddies while sharing an office at KROW.

Impressed by my less than conventional ads at Kahn's, the station had lured me by offering $100 a week, the extra $25 now paying for our maid Mabel Bridgewater to babysit while Sherwood kept selling freezers and refrigerators at Sears, Roebuck. Three years in the same job—unbelievable! Not that I had much opportunity to admire this incredible feat. Turning out a ton of ad copy at KROW, I was also trying to home-tutor our increasingly troubled daughter Sally, who was proving impossible to teach at school.

I thought, "I'll teach her math, goddammit," and I spent hours devising ways that might make it easier for her to learn, but it was no use. Sally was sweet, she was charming, and she was beautiful, but she also had brain damage—which we weren't yet aware of—and she just couldn't take in the information. It was heartbreaking. When her third-grade teacher at Edison Elementary came to our house and suggested that Sally should see the school psychol-

ogist, Sherwood flatly refused. He was probably afraid of anything
that might expose hereditary mental illness. After all, what would
it do to the venerable Diller name? He was aware of all the weird
things that had gone down with his family, but these were secrets
that he'd never talk about. So, I was up against a brick wall; Sherwood the brick wall. This was the story of my life—a wretched,
frustrating scenario which I'd try to forget while I was at work,
jazzing up the ads that were read live on air:

> *"At the Sea Wolf restaurant, the chefs are so temperamental
> that their wolf* du jour *has a psychiatrist in attendance at all
> times. . . ."*

I knew how to write catchy copy, baby, and I also had a knack for
making people laugh, a talent that didn't go unnoticed by Sherwood. He would watch TV and think I was funnier than the
comics on there, and he'd also observed how in-demand I was at
parties. So, ever keen to bring out the cash cow in me, he kept
pushing me towards a showbiz career, and I, in turn, began writing material based on my real-life experiences. One time at
home, after I had used vanity scissors to try plucking a turkey, it
looked like it was covered in little craters. Well, this lent itself to
a skit in which I lifted a turkey with tweezers, cut it with cuticle
scissors, stuffed it through the beak, and left the giblets inside because I didn't want to stick my hand up its ass.

I actually filmed this routine in October 1952, just three
months after my thirty-fifth birthday, utilizing an exhibition

kitchen at the General Appliance Company showroom in Oakland, a borrowed camera, and a $70 production budget assembled by several very supportive KROW colleagues. Jim Baker, one of Wanda Ramey's Hollywood contacts, served as the director, and I gave it my all in a full-length cocktail dress and chintzy lace apron. However, when *Phyllis Diller, the Friendly Homemaker* came back from the processors the sound and visuals weren't in sync, and with no money left to fix the problem my first great attempt at celluloid stardom had to be shelved. I haven't a clue what became of it.

A few months later, Wanda and my publicity apprentice, Don Arlett, threw a small bash at Buena Vista, a family-style Italian restaurant in San Francisco, and I remember turning up there in a threadbare prewar suit. That's how broke I was. Still, I put on a front by wearing black mesh stockings and a tatty faux-fur neck-piece while posing with a long black cigarette holder. Struggling and insecure, I was, as usual, the life of the party, trying to give the impression that everything was just A-okay. It wasn't, of course, but at least I sensed I was on an upward curve.

In January 1954, I was hired away from KROW by a lady named Alison Clark who ran a fashion advertising agency on Post Street in San Francisco. That got me across the bridge as well as into the TV and radio column of the *San Francisco Chronicle*, which quoted me saying, "I have had many offers in the past year. This is the only one involving a mink coat."

I didn't stay with Alison for very long. KSFO was the city's leading radio station, and the guy who ran it, Alan Torbet, had loved my work at KROW. So, that June, when he realized I was no longer with a competitor, Alan immediately hired me to pen funny ads as KSFO's Director of Promotion and Merchandising. He believed in me and he thought I was hot stuff, but that didn't mean he would let me do any broadcasting. To him I was still an office girl, even if *I* perceived myself differently.

Traveling to and from work on a bus, a tram, and a cable car, I would read *The Magic of Believing* and absorb what it was telling me. And eventually, armed with the courage as well as the belief, I also started writing down everything I wanted. As the book basically states, you wouldn't go to a grocery store without a grocery list, so why go throughout life without a list? By writing everything down you'll clear your head and clarify your goals. After all, what do you want out of life? Everyone will say, "I just want to be happy," but sometimes that isn't true. They want things like money and power that they might equate with happiness but that don't necessarily lead to it. It's terribly difficult to be honest with yourself. It means trying to be objective, whereas many, many people are *so* subjective . . . and boring, too.

So I had my notebook, and at a time when I was earning $5,000 a year, I drew a money bag with "$200,000" on it. I also wrote that I wanted to achieve this by way of music, writing, and humor, even though neither music nor humor applied to the job that I had. As Claude Bristol explained, you don't have to know how you're going to achieve your goals. Stop questioning, *start believing*. Once you do that, some truly unreal things start to happen. Now you've got the whole universe on your side. That's the magic. Believe in yourself and give yourself the power.

Just believe that there is genuine creative magic in believing—and magic there will be, for belief will supply the power which will enable you to succeed in everything you undertake. Back your belief with a resolute will and you become unconquerable—a master of men among men—yourself.

—Claude M. Bristol

You get to that point by throwing out all of your worry- and fear-related thoughts. What was in my mind all those years? Nothing but worry and fear. Now I started controlling my own mind and I had a system of thought that was positive. What's more, I treated people in that way. When I was very young I used to waste an awful lot of time letting others tell me their problems. But then I realized that it didn't do *them* any good, and it certainly depressed *me*. It was counterproductive, so from now on I had no time for people who'd use me as a sounding board. You know, "Spend a hundred bucks an hour and go see a psychiatrist. I don't work for free."

That's how I divested myself of these people who walk under a cloud. It's their own cloud which they've created, and it's always going to be there until they let the sun come out. You can't do it for them. I now don't have anyone in my life whom I don't want. I got rid of them. These included borrowers and users whom I really didn't have to put up with. In some cases, I'd become codependent. However, if you really want to get rid of some people, loan them money. *You'll never see them again.* I got rid of quite a few that way. I didn't realize it at the time, but looking back, that's what happened. They just disappeared.

Happiness, sought by many and found by few . . . is a matter entirely within ourselves; our environment and the everyday happenings of life have absolutely no effect on our happiness except as we permit mental images of the outside to enter our consciousness. Happiness is wholly independent of position, wealth, or material possessions. It is a state of mind which we ourselves have the power to control—and that control lies within our thinking.

—Claude M. Bristol

All our lives we're encumbered with stuff that's inflicted on us. People think they're helping, and in many cases they are, but a lot of what they have to offer is also a burden. For instance, my mother would never talk to anyone in her own voice. It was always a saying or a quote from Benjamin Franklin, Thomas Jefferson, William Shakespeare, or the Bible. "A stitch in time saves nine," "A penny saved is a penny earned"—I grew up on these quotes, but I learned to strip everything away while also trying to confront the subconscious thoughts that might be completely hamstringing me. Certain ideas that you've been given by your parents or teachers can paralyze you.

The Magic of Believing really made me think about my own life, because that's all any of us has. I became totally focused on my hopes and my objectives, and at the same time Sherwood kept saying, "You've got to become a comic, you've got to become a comic." Remember, he was always looking to come up with a product that could make money. Now I became the product. Still, despite my thinking he was out of his mind—which he was—the more he persisted, the more I began considering his advice.

I'd watch Sid Caesar on TV, as well as Milton Berle, Morey Amsterdam, Jonathan Winters, and various other comedians who appeared on those early shows coming out of the East Coast. They were all influences on me, as were those whom I'd heard on the radio since I was a teenager, and it was this love of humor that inspired much of my work at KSFO.

"If you are bothered by an old set, listen to The Don Sherwood Show. It sounds just as bad on a brand new set as it does on an old set. It's the only show that gives old set owners an even break."

"There are no prophets of doom on KSFO. Only the most cheerful news is good enough for KSFO's happy, happy listeners. When the weather reports are bad, KSFO's special earth-contour-hot-air-cold-air expert re-evaluates and edits the weather report to make it come out sunny and warmer."

"Want heartache? Mildred is crying because young Doctor Jerome removed the wrong kidney. He took Gertrude's kidney out, and it was Stephanie who needed it. . . . Now if you want to suffer, don't listen to KSFO because nothing depressing goes on there. KSFO's programs are just the most sweet."

If nothing else, my copy was out there and it was different. I remember one occasion when it produced such an incredible response that an advertiser felt obliged to visit the station and take a look at me. However, even though I was Alan Torbet's golden girl, I hated the guy who was put in charge of me when the station moved from the KPIX-TV building on Van Ness Avenue into the Fairmont Hotel on Mason Street. He probably resented me because he was a failed actor, and he'd give me "the arm" just as Italians do when they're telling you to fuck off—he had the charm of a skunk and the looks to match, yet he wasn't the only one who could be nasty.

I wore secondhand clothing to save money, and when I was in the john one day I heard somebody say, "I hope she doesn't wear that ratty fur coat again." They thought they were talking behind my back, but it was hurtful. Beforehand, when I'd worked at KROW, I had only one dress, and if I wore it two days in a row the accountant would say, "Didn't you go home?" I put up with an awful lot of crap. And do you know why? It was because I was a hard worker and I stuck out like a sore thumb no matter where I was. I knew I had to maneuver myself into a better situation.

While I was in the advertising department at Kahn's I had paid a visit to North Beach, the bohemian San Francisco neighborhood that was a haven for jazz clubs, strip joints, gay bars, and beatnik hangouts. Again, pushing me towards a career as a comic, Kahn's ad artist, Jenny Day, had told me to go there and see a funny woman named Jorie Remus performing at a club called the Purple Onion.

Jorie had turned out to be a willowy, sexy, French chanteuse-type with a husky voice, droll sense of humor, and haughty, heavily affected manner—a Gallic cross between Marlene Dietrich and Tallulah Bankhead, who'd address everyone as *"Daahling"* and assert that anything meeting with her approval was *"simply divine."* As I had watched her perform, interspersing torch songs with wry comments, it had sparked the idea that if she could do it, then perhaps I could, too. There had been no way of knowing it back then, but my stars were shifting into alignment.

Now fast-forward to my time at KSFO. One night after work I went to a jazz joint in downtown Oakland, where a man sitting next to me mentioned that he was Jorie Remus's drama coach. I said, "Whoa, you're just the person I'm looking for!" Out of that entire city, I'd managed to sit next to one of the few guys who could really get me started. His name was Lloyd Clark and guess who else he had coached—Maya Angelou. Born Marguerite Johnson, this celebrated poet and author was then a calypso dancer and singer, and Lloyd had invented her name, taught her how to make an entrance, and helped her become a big, big success. I couldn't believe my luck.

I told Lloyd about the comic and musical turns that I'd occasionally perform at parties and small charity events, and how everyone was now insisting that I should turn professional. I said, "Would you work with me? I'd like to audition."

"Do you write your own material?" he inquired.

"Sure," I replied, aware that the audition had already begun. "Before a party, my girlfriends often call and ask me to come up with some jokes about the cooking, the cleaning, whatever. They love that kind of stuff. I've got a fair bit . . ."

"Then we should get together and run through it," Lloyd interjected without a moment's hesitation.

I'd made it to first base. Several nights later, the two of us met at my house after work, and during the next few days, we also spoke quite a lot over the phone. Concluding that I had the talent and the personality to succeed, Lloyd agreed to help develop my act, and soon we were calling each other constantly with new jokes or ones that we'd found in magazines. The deal was for him to get $5 an hour if we so much as talked, and I ran up quite a bill because, with six people to support at home and a phone that was continually getting disconnected, I just couldn't pay him. I said, "It's on faith. You're gonna get whatever I owe you," and eventually he would.

Lloyd was a nightclub person who had tremendous connections to the Purple Onion. Suave, dark-haired, pencil thin, and overtly gay, he was there every night with a huge white mound who happened to be his wife. Also named Marguerite, this heavyset blonde's cloying, soft-spoken demeanor really didn't match a face that could stop a clock, yet she fussed and fawned over her prissy husband and he just lapped it up. Lloyd spoke in a clipped, tight-lipped manner that reminded me of the actor Clifton Webb—to him, everyone was "my dear"—and I quickly realized that he knew the entire North Beach scene like the back of his hand.

During the mid-fifties, this "Little Italy" neighborhood located next to Chinatown was the most exciting part of the city. Packed with an eclectic combination of locals and tourists, and pulsating to the music that drifted out of clubs and bars while *cacciatore* and *puttanesca* scents filled the air, North Beach was, in a word, *alive*. And it also served as a talent magnet and cultural free-for-all during an era dominated by conservative values.

Visitors could see comic Mort Sahl at the hungry i and a young singer named Johnny Mathis at Ann's 440; check out the belly dancers at 12 Adler or the strippers doing their thing in any of the joints along Broadway; take in some jazz and a drag show at Finnochio's; attend beat poetry readings at Lawrence Ferlinghetti's City Lights bookstore; or watch the poets themselves getting sauced at the adjacent Vesuvio Café. The diagonal thoroughfare for much of this activity was Columbus Avenue, and there at No. 140, in a basement below the sidewalk, was the Purple Onion.

Keith Rockwell had opened this tiny venue for Jorie Remus after giving up his part-ownership in Enrico Banducci's hungry i, that smoke-filled "hungry intellectual" wine cellar whose brick wall served as a backdrop for many of the era's most famous comedians. Jorie had performed at the hungry i, and Keith, who was her bass player, absolutely adored her. However, Banducci didn't think she was anything special, so Keith had gone across the street and opened the Purple Onion to ensure that she still had a stage.

I, of course, had never been *on* a nightclub stage, so while Lloyd Clark coached me and wrote for me, I looked for ways to get some semi-pro experience. Aware that the Red Cross often recruited both amateurs and professionals to entertain hospitalized servicemen, I volunteered and was sent to the San Francisco Army Base's Presidio Hospital. There my first audience consisted of four guys in four beds who looked like they'd rather be left alone than have some ugly broad singing and telling them stories. The poor things, I probably delayed their recovery. Nevertheless, my eldest son Peter, who was now a fabulous banjo player, performed alongside me, and that gig got me started before I set about polishing the material that I had been using for years on an amateur basis. As it turned out, my second gig was at the very same hospital, although this time it took place in the psychiatric ward. I guess they figured I had found my true audience.

Over the course of a year, I performed at church halls, women's clubs, and other small places, and I also appeared in a production titled *The Poets' Follies of 1955.* This was a literary and musical revue, written and coproduced by composer-pianist-poet-painter Weldon Kees, featuring jazz musicians, local actors in a series of short sketches, and writers such as Ferlinghetti reading assorted works. It was staged on weekends in venues around town, such as the Theater Arts Colony and Berkeley Little Theater, and it was so good that it garnered a glowing review in *The New York Times*.

I was initially cast in a very small role—I remember portraying some high-society dame with a tennis racket whose lines included "I think I'll go out and hit a few balls"—but it kept growing with every reincarnation of the show, to the point where I appeared in all three acts of coproducer Michael Grieg's drama *The Three Bottles.* That illustrates what I had: natural ascendancy (even if the aforementioned *Times* review did refer to me as Phyllis Dillard).

Unfortunately, Weldon Kees was a very talented but very disturbed man. I realized this when I visited his tiny house and saw a huge, totally black painting that he had done. Divorced from his alcoholic, mentally disturbed wife, and deeply depressed, he would throw himself off the Golden Gate Bridge in the summer of 1955.

Earlier, in February of that year, I finally felt ready to take the plunge at the Purple Onion. In those days you had to get the job, because there was no such thing as "open mic night." There was an open *audition* on the last Saturday of every month, and anybody of any age and any color could try out. The person in charge of choosing talent was Barrymore Drew, an older gay guy who had been a radio star in Chicago and a member of the famous Barrymore theatrical family. He now owned a tenth of the club and took care of the lights, the sound, the announcements, the greetings at the door, and nurturing the new, green performers. Tall and elegant, although he always wore sandals, Barry was a wonderful housemother as well as a gentle person with a great sense of humor. He once told me, "I was always torn between whether I wanted to be Mary Pickford or Douglas Fairbanks."

Lloyd Clark set up a special audition for me—not one where I had to go in on a Saturday—and, on the big day, I dressed gorgeous. I wore a tight black cotton evening dress with one shoulder off, and beautiful high-heeled shoes with rhinestone straps that I'd refer to as "whore shoes," a play on horseshoes—I had lots of teeny little jokes. However, the people who were supposed to be watching and listening to me ordered Chinese food over the phone, and they didn't appear to pay a bit of attention during the ten or twelve minutes that I went through my routine.

It was a family-owned business, and the family was auditioning me: old Mama Rockwell, who'd greet people at the door with Barry Drew; her son Keith; daughter Virginia; Virginia's husband, Bud Steinhoff; and Don Currie, who was the manager and bartender. There they all were while I was doing my thing, ordering butterfly shrimps with fried rice before completing my humiliation with a curt "Thank you." You see, they had just hired a comic, Milt Kamen, a French horn player from New York whose material was actually far too avant-garde and way-out for many people to follow. He had the job and the Purple Onion had a policy: It always hired a singer, a comic, and a self-contained act— when the self-contained act went on, the pianist could have his union time off. It was a matter of business. As Milt Kamen was already the comic, it was hard to figure out why I'd even auditioned.

Given my typically dire home life, this failure was a black alley, a brick wall, a closed door, but I didn't let it discourage me. Instead, I quit my job at KSFO in order to become an unemployed comic. It was my grand gesture. When I told my boss that I was quitting, he said, "No, I'm gonna give you a leave of absence," but I said, "I don't want a leave of absence. Fill my job. I won't be back." Thanks to *The Magic of Believing,* I somehow knew that it would work and that I could do it. Nevertheless, when the radio station threw a little goodbye party for me, the jerk in charge inscribed my card with "A Scar Is Born." Fortunately for him, I can't remember his name, but I can still picture what he looked like. He was an ugly little asshole, and when you have an alias like that, who needs a name?

Milt Kamen, meanwhile, was homesick for New York. He

missed his friends and he couldn't find a bagel in San Francisco. So, when somebody called and offered him a two-week radio job back East, he begged the Purple Onion to give him some time off and finally they figured, "What the hell. Who was that chick who auditioned here a couple of weeks ago?"

I received a call on a Friday night, asking, "Phyllis, can you open on Monday?" I said, "Absolutely." Once again, it was all about timing, baby, and it always is. However, it's also a long way between the living room and the spotlight, even in a little club, and I had to go straight there.

I made my professional debut on Monday, March 7, 1955, wearing a dark, sleeveless Jonathan Logan cotton dress that had been bought for me by my good friend, great supporter, and former KROW colleague Wanda Ramey, who was now hosting the daytime news on KPIX-TV. All of my friends attended that first Purple Onion performance, but half of the audience was still there for the second show and I only had one show's worth of material. That was a nightmare. Even if you hear the same person perform a song seventy-three times you'll always applaud at the end, but you can only laugh once at the same joke. A comic lives on every line. After that I wrote a second show so fast, enabling me to deal with the overlap if I did two or three performances.

I'd sing my trusty "Indian Love Call" and a cabaret number entitled "I'd Rather Cha-Cha Than Eat," as well as a German lieder accompanied by a phony translation and a spoof of Gian Carlo Menotti's Christmas opera *Amahl and the Night Visitors*, imitating the singer Yma Sumac while beating on an oatmeal box. I guess I wouldn't have gotten out of San Francisco with that act, but it was hard to ignore my background in classical music.

Indeed, just two days after my debut the *San Francisco Examiner* noted that "Phyllis Diller has given up radio to follow what she calls 'her secret heart.' Singing, that is. 'I was discussing this with my bathtub the other day,' confides the bright redhead, 'and he says I have one of the finest tile-plated voices this side of the Crane factory.' She opens at the Purple Onion this week."

Not that all of my material was music-based. I'd talk about an ad in the *Examiner* for a $100,000 sable coat that you needed an appointment to see, and I would put on a hat with feathers that was exactly like one on the cover of *Vogue* and say, "You'd be surprised what this goes for . . . before the legs are removed." It was very light humor, but terribly chic. Oh *God*, was I chic! I was born loving fashion, and I still love fashion. It *turns me on*, and when you feel that way about something it's real easy to make fun of it.

A bright new face has turned up at the Purple Onion. It belongs to Phyllis Diller, who recently has been devastating audiences in the Poets' Follies. She resigned her job at KSFO to try her pixilated comedy on nightclub audiences. We predict good things for her.
—San Francisco Chronicle, *March 12, 1955*

My confidence and my delivery both improved over the course of those first two weeks at the Onion, and by the time that Milt Kamen returned from his gig in New York the club owners were confused. They wanted to keep whoever was going to make it. This guy Milt always brought out notes from his pocket whereas I was a pro right from the start. There were things that I would never stoop to, and I would sweat blood before I'd bring out a note. I thought it was unprofessional for him to do that. However, in the end, the owners did something unique in the history of the club: they kept us both.

Housing 170 seats that were basically director's chairs, the Purple Onion was an intimate joint. To the left, after you walked down a steep flight of sixteen steps from the street, was the bar— a very active gay bar—and up about four steps on that side was a booth with wooden bench seats. Then, on the right, there was a dressing room the size of a postage stamp—imagine the Kingston Trio folk group having to change alongside me, a thirty-seven-year-old Alameda housewife in a bustier, before bustiers were in. It was so damp in there that the mice would scamper around the mold. One night I even caught a baby mouse and took it home to replace our pet canary which had just died. I was *so* resourceful.

Directly opposite the main staircase was the "stage," which was about four feet wide, six feet deep, flat to the floor, and in the center of a terrific room whose asymmetry lent itself to a wonderfully warm atmosphere, reflective of the family ownership. Virginia Steinhoff worked her tail off, kneeling to get the drink orders so that she was never blocking anybody's view, Barry Drew operated the one light amid the darkness, and if anybody stepped out of line, by God, they were thrown out. In fact, Barry would often turn away loudmouthed millionaires until they sobered up.

It was that kind of place, catering to the best interests of the patrons and the performers.

The grand piano, which had a piece of driftwood with purple onions attached to it, was in front of a brick wall, and the performers stood on a rug where they were picked up by an overhead mic. That overhead mic was the secret of a great show, because in this little venue the word was *live* and nothing got in the way. When I danced on the piano, I was totally free of encumbrance, whereas I would experience culture shock when I'd get to my next job and actually have to deal with a microphone. To this day, none of the clubs go with the overhead mic, and I can't figure out why. They always stick that damned thing in your hand, and it wasn't until the wireless mic was introduced many years later that I'd regain my freedom onstage.

At the start of my career, friends and former coworkers would attend my shows and encourage me in any way they could, and I also enjoyed plenty of support from the local press and media. My former KSFO radio colleague Don Sherwood hosted TV shows such as *Pop Club* on KGO and *San Francisco Tonight* on KPIX, and it was thanks to him that I began making small-screen appearances as early as April 1955. Then again, one of my first newspaper features was a May 17 *San Francisco Chronicle* piece by Marjorie Trumbull titled "Phyllis Diller—She Knows of Love and Laughter."

This described my background as an ad copywriter, my family of five children who were cared for by an "obviously understanding husband"—*obviously*—and my "extremely funny, musical act," which had the columnist "laughing out loud in sheer delight." It was good publicity and Marjorie Trumbull was one of my early champions, penning several articles about my "peculiarly zany, original, uninhibited brand of humor."

The next month, I was mentioned in an *Alameda Times-Star* ad feature that promoted a "Big TV Talent Show" to herald the "Grand Opening" of a Freeman Markets grocery store—on the way up I did anything and everything to be out there, to be known, to be seen. The paper ran a photo of me with mistress of ceremonies Wanda Ramey, and I was evidently making an impression in that little town because I was billed as "Alameda's Own Comedy Star" who would be "performing some of her original skits." Well, original they certainly were.

Lloyd Clark was writing for me and he wrote *incredible* stuff. It was Lloyd who provided me with the most brilliant, devastating parody of Eartha Kitt singing "Monotonous" in *New Faces of 1952,* where she started at one end of the stage and literally squirmed her way across four chaise lounges as a bored femme fatale, grumbling, "T. S. Eliot writes books for me, King Farouk's on tenterhooks for me, Sherman Billingsley even cooks for me! MONOTONOUS!" Lloyd transformed this into a number entitled "Ridiculous," and I'd perform it on top of the piano in a black leotard, a cross between a cat and a snake, slithering all over the place while imitating Eartha's voice and attitude.

"Life amounts to nothing but a hill of beans.
It's only repetitious stuff, the same tired scenes . . .
RIDICULOUS!"

Lloyd was a very sophisticated writer and his words reflected this. It was a wonderful number, written specifically for me by a guy who loved me and who had been working with me. Yet, there was a downside. His material was all very chichi and I soon found that the public wanted something completely different, more along the lines of a truthful and honest spoofing of every-day life. This was what I focused on writing, while also using his material, until one day I finally said, "Why do you always throw out my ideas and keep your own?"

You see, I was getting into my thing: the husband and the kids and the cooking and the house. That's what I needed to do—it came right out of my soul and it worked. That's how I'd made my friends and colleagues laugh for all these years, and I could see that it was having the same effect on audiences. So, I went with that and split from Lloyd.

Had I stayed with him and gone in his direction I wouldn't be writing this book, and the same might be said if I hadn't taken Keith Rockwell's advice to smile less and be more hostile on-stage. Comedy is mock hostility. If the hostility ever looks real, you won't make it, but I was so nervous, wanting people to like me and be my friends, that the lines I was delivering required more antagonism. And Keith was right to point this out. Later on, I would learn more about showing mock hostility when per-forming at larger venues in the round, where the audience sur-rounds you on all sides.

As a performer you often need to feel secure and have the op-tion of exiting stage left or stage right, whereas when you're sur-rounded by people you're trapped, you're vulnerable, and you're theirs. Now, if you have the ability or the warmth or whatever it takes to deal with that, it's a wonderful thing. It's the most power you can feel. For me it would be a piece of cake, and I'd learn to enhance my performances in the round by actually watching the way Don Rickles paced himself to show hostility, scanning the audience and looking behind him as if to say, "They're after me. Oh my God, cover for me." I'd think, "I've got to learn to do that," and when I'd succeed in learning, it would free me. Improvisation can be a wonderful thing.

Early on, it was thanks to an ad-lib that I developed the character of Fang, that incompetent, half-witted husband who evolved out of my love for Bob Newhart's "Driving Instructor" routine; a monologue that detailed a catastrophic lesson with a bungling broad. I was so crazy about it that I decided to write a driving bit for myself in which I described how, as the stereotypical, disaster-prone woman behind the wheel, "You have to call home and tell 'Old Fang Face' about the accident."

> I said, "Hello, I've had a little accident at the corner of Post and Geary," and he said, "Post and Geary don't cross." I said, "They do now."

That was my first driving joke, and thereafter I wrote many, many bits concerning my misadventures in the car. Meanwhile, I also shortened Old Fang Face to Fang Face and came up with jokes like "Well, what would *you* call a man with one tooth two-inches long? I met him at a cocktail party. I thought it was a cigarette. I tried to light it. He was so drunk, he tried to smoke it . . ." This went on and on and on, and it was after several months that I finally reduced the name to Fang.

Oh, that man is so stupid. He was stranded for six hours on an escalator when the power failed. A priest tried to talk him down . . . At the mall, he went up to a map that said "You Are Here," and he wondered how they knew . . . Having decided that blondes have more fun, he bleached his hair and asked me for a divorce.

If only. Just as I was the antithesis of the happy and attractive fifties housewife, so Fang flipped the image of the capable husband who was king of his castle, and I soon realized he was a beloved character. No one knew I was living with an agoraphobic sex tyrant who couldn't socialize and rarely held down a job. And not until the year of my retirement would I be aware that my stage act was actually a form of therapy. Boy, did I need it.

Five

THE BOTTOM OF
THE BARREL

During my initial year at the Purple Onion, the first show every night played to a Gray Line tour from Alabama, Florida, Idaho, Illinois, Indiana, Michigan, Montana, Ohio . . . you name it. I got a shot at audiences from all over the country who probably looked around that dark, musty basement and thought they were in a den of iniquity. And that was a wonderful training, because my goal was to entertain anyone, anywhere, from three years old to a hundred and three.

I was constantly coming up with new material and different characters to impersonate: a fortune-teller, a grooming consultant, even a gangster's moll who, with a cigarette dangling out of her mouth, would say, "We're gonna heist an underwear factory . . . I don't want no slips." That was a *stupid* joke, but the delivery made it funny. Everything has to be impeccably timed when you're going for laughs, so thank God I was born with great timing. This had been evident since the age of three, when I could sit at a piano and play harmony. And I had also learned from my daddy, listening to his spiel as he sold insurance and observing how he would allow the clients to think after he had stopped talking. Nevertheless, timing is natural, it's not something you can be taught. If a stage director tells you, "Count to three and then do such-and-such," forget it. Every audience is different. You just have to go with the flow and rely on your instincts, because it always takes people a moment to digest a joke before they'll laugh.

My own laugh is the real thing and I've had it all my life. My father used to call me the laughing hyena. Like a yawn or a mood, it's infectious, and that's a great plus for a comic, but I don't just turn it on like some of today's performers. In fact, during the early stages of my career it was a nervous laugh. I was scared out of my mind. The sweat ran down my back into my shoes and it was so strong with body acids that it ate the leather lining. That's what is known as flop sweat—it doesn't mean you're flopping; you're just petrified—and I had man-sized coat shields in my dress to try to absorb it.

Another thing I occasionally suffered from was the trots. Performers often get the trots on opening night, and that's what happened to me one time when I was opening for Anthony Newley back East. I made a dash for the john in the trailer we were sharing but I couldn't get in. How was I to know he always took a shower before the show? I'm telling you, this whole process wasn't easy. It would take me years to feel totally at home onstage. I'd have wonderful material and just ride that material. And besides, when you feel the love and approval of people who laugh and clap as soon as you walk on, there's no reason to sweat or lose control. These days I'm *as cool as a cucumber* . . . especially since I don't work.

I love to go to the doctor. Where else would a man look at me and say, "Take off your clothes"?

I never intended to be dirty, but a lot of people would read innuendo into what I said. For instance, when I'd impersonate supper-club entertainer Hildegarde singing "The Little Things You Used to Do," I'd sexily go all the way up the octave just repeating that line and comment, "He was a very small man." I wasn't referring to his privates, I was simply quipping that he was a small thinker, a shallow person, but a lot of people would hear that and say, "Oh *boy*, is she dirty." I wasn't aware of this at the time. I was so innocent that it took me years to learn that I was dirty. And early on, I purposely never watched other comedians perform because I didn't want to copy *anyone*.

I wanted to become *me*, totally me. The more me, the better. I instinctively knew this and I was right. My attitude, my material, and me—those were the components that distinguished me from the rest of the field right from the start. Everybody who walks onstage has an attitude, but whereas Mort Sahl had a su-

perior and somewhat condescending attitude, my audiences rec-
ognized that with me they were only encountering mock hostility. I wanted to make them laugh, I wanted to make them happy.
I had a spirit, baby, I was strong, and it was almost as if there was
a field of light around me. When your whole body is electricity,
you can use it, and I was able to capitalize on material that no
one else had in their artillery.

For instance, everybody has always assumed that Sherwood
was Fang—even Sherry assumed that he was Fang, and he *loved*
it. Oh honey, he *wanted to be* Fang! Years later, he'd receive a letter in St. Louis with no address listed, not even a town, just the
name Fang, and he'd also have stationery with only a fang logo.
He was in heaven. At last he had been endowed with the importance that he'd always wanted. Now he could go into a bar and
say, "I'm Fang, do you wanna buy me a drink?" However, in my
mind Sherry was definitely *not* Fang, and I made that very clear.
Fang was just a mythical spouse, the first character that I developed, and forever my favorite. In his wake, I created numerous
others, like his mother, Moby Dick, and sister, Captain Bligh.

*Moby Dick's dress size is junior missile. We didn't have a sunken
living room until she arrived. When she takes her girdle off, her
feet disappear. Someday I'd like to slit that girdle open and watch
her spread to death. . . . Talk about old—her social security
number is 2! The only reason she wasn't on Noah's Ark was because they couldn't find another animal that looked like her. . . .
God, she's ugly! When she blew her nose downtown, the con-*

struction crew broke for lunch. . . . You should hear her sing. She hit high C and spayed the dog. . . .

This was *my* material, unique to me because it stemmed from my own life. Now that I realized I could create characters, I kept doing so, and this would continue right up until the end of my standup career. In fact, the last character I ever found—and I could kick myself for finding her so late—was my sexy sister:

It took the driving instructor two days to teach her how to sit up in a car. . . . She was the original meter maid—all you had to do was meet her, you got her made. . . . She broke her ankle in a glove compartment. . . . She spent more time with the team than the coach. . . . She told me she wanted a white wedding; I told her, "You'd better pray for snow . . ."

The last thing I'd learn, well into my career, was how to get *on*, how to say hello, how to get in with the audience. God, I experimented with everything. The worst thing in the world is the amateur comic who asks, "Anybody here from Cleveland?" Oh, *Jesus.* "Are you having a good time?" How do they know if they're having a good time? They've only just arrived. That's a cheap way to get a reaction, and it's also the worst possible move, creating an opening for the audience to talk. If they take control with that question you'll never get it back. And besides, how dare you come out and ask them a question? You're supposed to be giving a show and it should start with some form of hello. It was at New York's Bon Soir nightclub during the early sixties that the comic Charlie Manna gave me the greatest advice about how to get on: quickly tell five of your hottest jokes and then run with them. Get the audience laughing for real, don't make it a phony deal.

"The Purple Onion is pleased, proud, and absolutely terrified to present the one and, God help us, the only dingy, dilly, delirious doll from Donner Pass, Phyllis Diller!"

I performed six nights a week at the Purple Onion—we had Sundays off—and although there were normally four shows, we did six on one particular Saturday night during my first year. That meant the customers were brought in fast, we did short shows, and they were then moved out just as quickly. The first show went on at eight, the last one ended at two, and each featured three acts. At that time, these included Maya Angelou, Milt Kamen, singers Ketty Frierson and Lloyd Sparks, and "rhythm stylists" Jackie Cain and Roy Krall, so what a variety people got.

Larry Tucker, who would later write the screenplay for *I Love You, Alice B. Toklas*, took over from Don Currie as the Onion's manager and bartender, and one of his dear friends was the comic Dick Gautier, who worked at the hungry i. After that job was over, Gautier wanted to work at the Purple Onion, and in order for that to happen Larry decided to get me out of there. So, he talked with Keith Rockwell and Keith fired me. However, thanks to *The Magic of Believing*, I didn't respond as expected.

"That's okay," I told him. " I really don't need this job to make my way in the world of comedy. You gave me my start and that's enough. Don't worry about me, I'll be fine."

Used to guys putting their fists through walls while yelling, screaming, and using a lot of bad words, Keith was so impressed by my reaction that within a week he had un-fired me. He then told Larry Tucker and Dick Gautier about this, and those sly boys quickly realized they'd been foiled.

I mean, here's what Dick Gautier was like: the performance area at the Purple Onion was so small that some audience members were practically onstage with you, sitting in your light, and Dick came and sat in that front chair one night during one of my shows before the firing and he never smiled. Instead he just glowered at me for the entire twenty minutes, shooting daggers, and that was done on purpose. A similar thing happened several years later when, on my second night at the Bon Soir, the owner bumped me up to top of the bill in place of Jimmy Komack. He had worked there for years as the headlining comic, and his reaction was to have his wife come in with a party of eight, sit in my light directly in front of the stage, and never laugh or smile once during my performance. It was so mean and so pathetic, but by then I was stronger. They thought they could keep the whole room quiet, but it didn't work.

Another time, again early in my career at the Purple Onion, it was nearing Christmas and Keith asked me to leave so that he could hire Jane and Gordon Connell. Graduates of the Berkeley School of Drama, they had appeared as a musical-comedy duo at the Onion before I arrived on the scene, and they were very hot stuff. That having been said, they were also close friends of mine—Gordon had been my pianist, and he had rehearsed with me before I ever got the job. He and Jane were based in New York, but now they wanted to come back and work at the Purple Onion so they could visit their family in California.

I said, "Keith, I have five children. It's going to be Christmas at my house, too." Once again, he just couldn't get rid of me. And in August 1955 I was given top billing when Maya Angelou left, joining the traveling company of *Porgy and Bess* for an international tour.

Initially, the Purple Onion paid me $60 a week, which was below scale. That covered food and gas for the car, but I still remember putting an ad in the newspaper one Sunday and selling my mother's diamond engagement ring. That *really* upset me. Sherwood had met a guy who was supposedly making a fortune selling encyclopedias, so he'd quit Sears, Roebuck to do the same and, of course, he never sold a single copy. He probably didn't even knock on anyone's door. Then, someone else whom he'd met at Sears got him into a training program with the Prudential Life Insurance Company. The program was extensive and the trainees were paid while they were taking the course, but even though most were hired at the end of it, Sherry was not among them. Again, he was out of work.

Unfortunately, none of this diminished his appetite for sex; really *terrible* sex. And Fremont Drive is where things got out of hand. We had twin beds on either side of the room and he'd simply walk over and get on top of me. Oh God, it was a nightmare, and when I wasn't gritting my teeth, I was usually fighting him off. I would run and try to hide in the garage, hide in the car, hide in the doghouse; anything to get away from him. Once, when I said no, he picked me up and accidentally hit my head against a wall, blackening an eye and spilling blood, but at least I got out of it that night. I'm telling you, if our marriage amounted to a lot of date rape, then Sherwood Diller was the worst sex offender who ever lived.

Never go to bed mad. Stay up and fight.

On another occasion, I returned from a show at about two-thirty one morning, smelled smoke, went up to the bedroom, and his mattress was on fire. He had fallen asleep with a cigarette in his hand, and if I hadn't arrived home at that moment he and the children would have burned to death. As it was, I helped him throw the mattress out of the window and life staggered on as abnormal.

Our house had three bedrooms—Peter, being the eldest kid, slept in one, and Sally, Suzanne, Stephanie, and little Perry were in the other. I loved to spend time in there every night, playing creative games, putting them in a happy mood, trying to get them to bed; yet Sherwood would invariably stand at the foot of the stairway and yell at me, "Get down here!" If I did go and ask why, I'd discover there was no reason. He simply wouldn't allow me to be with them as long as I wanted. That really hurt. So what if he was afraid to be alone? His selfishness was some-thing else.

During the day, I'd give our kids plenty of freedom to play. I just loved to see them having fun, and if they wrecked the living room that was all right with me. You see, I was a *lousy* house-keeper, so I really wasn't concerned about the mess. I'd always get out of doing the chores by practicing on the piano, but that wasn't the case for our neighbor. Whereas her kids practically lived at our house, our children were never allowed inside her home because she wanted to keep it spotless and tidy. Got the picture? Still, it was thanks to this woman that I came up with another character for my jokes: that perfect housewife, Mrs. Clean. Oh, I *hated* her . . .

She not only washes the windows, she irons them. She waxes her driveway. Her husband got drunk one night, passed out on the coffee table, and she came down the next morning and polished him to death. If there is anything to reincarnation, that bitch will come back as a Brillo pad.

In early 1956, I made yet another addition to my routine, reading a "Dear Abby" letter while changing the words—the ad-vice column of Pauline "Abby" Phillips began appearing in the *San Francisco Chronicle* around this time, and she'd come to the club because she knew I was using her stuff. Reading from the newspaper, I'd say, "Dear Abby, our father who is—this is not a prayer—in his fifties, has been taking out a woman several years his junior. My sisters and I do not think he should be going out with anyone. This woman is probably after what he has got."

The reply? "Dear Anna, Thelma, and Tetra-ethel, Mind your own business. Your father and I are having one helluva time!"

The end of my year-long run at the Onion coincided with the owners launching a venue in Los Angeles and asking me to do the opening shows along with the darling black singer Ketty Frierson. That meant I'd have to spend four months in L.A. while Sherwood would remain with the kids and do the Mr. Mom thing in Alameda. Hardly an enticing thought, but this was the deal if I wanted to sustain career momentum. I should have known from the get-go it would be more trouble than it was worth.

On the eve of my departure for Los Angeles, Sherry faked a heart attack. That man was in a constant state of anxiety. It had been *his* idea for me to get into this business, and you don't become a big star staying in one town. You eventually have to go somewhere else, but the day before I left for L.A. he was having a coronary and I wasn't buying it. I called the doctor, who was a personal friend, and he told us to come to his office. Then, when we walked in, the first thing he said was, "Are you two having some kind of trouble?" He knew exactly what was going on. The doc asked me to leave and that's what I did, setting off for Los Angeles in a small one-engine plane while Sherry underwent his "examination."

Still, when I was away he did actually look after the kids. I don't know how he fed them, I don't know how he managed, but I'd return home every two weeks and the house would be clean and everyone would look fine. By now, our sixteen-year-old son Peter was living on his own in L.A. and attending Hollywood High School. He had liked the city when spending time there with Aunt Jessie a decade earlier, and now he was back, doing very well at Hollywood High and renting a room with an outside entrance on Poinsettia Avenue, just off Sunset Boulevard, where a little old lady watched over him.

When I arrived in town to open the new Purple Onion in the summer of 'fifty-six, I lived in a tiny house behind the club, which was located on a crummy part of Sunset. My place had a little kitchen, a little living room, and a little bedroom, but Peter and I would often get together there and take the opportunity to have more of a mother-son relationship than we'd ever had in a home with five children. We would talk for hours about his schoolwork and what he intended to do after graduation, and we'd also listen to records and indulge our passion for jazz. He was a great kid, a very thoughtful person, and I adored having him around.

The L.A. Purple Onion was just another room and things there were really tough for me. On many occasions my act didn't work, nobody was in the club, and I'd cut my material apart after the show, put it on the floor, and sit in the middle and cry. I'd try to figure out how to revise it and make it funnier, but I felt lost. At that time, L.A. was certainly not a club town—and it still isn't—so the venue never succeeded. Many people here get up at five a.m. to work their tails off in television or in the movies, and they're not going to hang out at little nighttime places that are open until two in the morning. What with all of the flowers and the sunshine, they live like farmers, and when it's dark they go to bed.

This is the only town in the world where you can buy rhinestone corn pads and women wear pants whether they should or not. I was walking down Hollywood Boulevard the other day behind a fat woman in pants, and it looked like two small boys fighting under a blanket. Wanting to look like a native, I bought a very tight pair of pants, only to find out that my skin was too loose. I was late to my first appointment because it took me two hours to stuff my gray flannel skin into my blue suede slacks.

At a loss for what to do, I decided to sparkle things up. With my dark hair I looked like the typical woman next door, but people don't have to visit a club to see the woman next door. I'd always thought that girls who wore sequins had bad taste, yet it wasn't long before I was sparkling like them, reflecting light with a platinum-blond hairdo that was aimed at grabbing *everybody's* attention. Without a doubt, I was born to be in that spotlight, even if it had taken Sherwood Diller to make me realize it . . . well, him and poverty.

It was during my stint at the L.A. Purple Onion that I made my first appearance on national television. A couple of people who were terribly impressed with my talent and my material had contacts to TV producer John Guedel, and thanks to them I was granted three in-depth interviews before being accepted as a contestant on the NBC game show *You Bet Your Life*. Hosted by

Groucho Marx, this featured question-and-answer rounds and cash prizes, yet the contestants were primarily selected for their ability to deal with Groucho's trademark barbs. I thought it might serve as the perfect showcase for me.

I was teamed with a nuclear physicist, and we both missed out on the question "What is the newest democracy in Africa?" The answer was Ghana, but neither of us knew it. He was too involved with physics and I was too involved with comedy, so we weren't following the news. Still, my only reason for appearing on that Thursday night show was to push myself and gain widespread exposure, and I'm sure Groucho knew this. Therefore, when I informed both him and the viewers that I was a comic, he invited me to tell some jokes. For me this was a big deal, but unfortunately it all came to nothing because of one glaring problem: trying to ensure that I didn't say anything too offensive, I just wasn't funny.

I went to this analyst. He's helped me a great deal. In fact, I am so much better now, I get to sit up.

Groucho was completely nonplussed and who could blame him? He looked at me as if I were a turd. No one had ever seen that kind of look on his face before: "What is it? *Why* is it? What is it doing here on my show?" I must have been one of the first people to ever render him speechless. Of course, after I became famous that appearance would be rerun about four thousand times, but what a dud! I still saw TV as the way forward, yet I'd have to do a whole lot better if I wanted it to help break me na-

My parents, Frances Ada Romshe Driver and Perry Marcus Driver, on their wedding day in 1909.

My daddy, who loved cars, behind the wheel of his right-hand-drive Paige, one of the first automobiles in Lima, Ohio. Looking around him, Mother has his ear as a professional backseat driver.

"Bye, baby bunting, Daddy's gone a-hunting . . ." My father built this sled for me, covered in red, white, and blue bunting. (Note the stars and stripes.) I was just eight months old.

Eighteen months old—no wonder I love jewelry and books. I started early. This dress was made by my mother, who made all my clothes through high school. To this day, all my clothing is designer/custom-made.

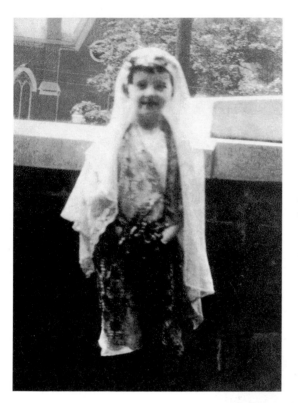

Six years old, in the roof garden atop the Electron Apartments in Lima, Ohio. The wedding garb is my own design—old lace curtains. Note the bouquet. In the background is the Presbyterian Church.

Twenty years old, on the Krehbiel Bridge of the Bluffton College campus. The cotton print formal—again, my own design—allowed for a bare midriff. I was way ahead.

A delicate ninety-pounder
with a beautiful firstborn,
Peter (b. 1940).

At home in Alameda, California, in 1952 with (*left to right*) Peter, Sally, Suzanne, Stephanie, and Perry. I was a copywriter at radio station KROW, and the shot was arranged for me as a favor by the station's photographer, yet Sherwood refused to show up.

My professional debut, March 7, 1955, at the
Purple Onion in San Francisco.

A gangster moll at the
Purple Onion.

I had no idea why the audience laughed when I put on my glove.
My coach and writer, Lloyd Clark, said, "Don't ask, just do it."
I had heard the word, but I didn't know about the finger.

A 1961 family shot taken in Chicago, where I was performing at Mister Kelly's nightclub. Back row (*left to right*): Suzanne, Peter, and Sally. Front row: Perry, Sherwood, me, and Stephanie.

With Barbra Streisand at the Bon Soir in New York City, September 1960.

With Warde Donovan Tatum on our wedding day, October 7, 1965, at the Pacific Palisades home of his brother, Disney exec Donn Tatum.

Grady Sutton, a veteran of more than two hundred movies, most notably four with W. C. Fields, portrayed Sturgis the butler in my 1966 ABC comedy series, *The Pruitts of Southampton*.

Bob liked my old face.
Eight on the Lam, 1967.

Playboy shot it and shelved it.

I made it! Onstage at the St. James Theatre, Broadway,
next door to Sardi's, 1970.

Before and after.

Having a ball on NBC's *The Dean Martin Show*.
Dean was the *only* person who ever played Fang.

With my true love, Bob Hastings,
and the Reagans.

tionally. And I'd also need to appear on a show that would allow me to perform much more of my set material.

In the meantime, I was suffering through my run at the L.A. Purple Onion, and a letter that my friends at the *San Francisco Chronicle* published in September 1956 attested to this:

> *I still have the problem of people telling me what's wrong with my act. During the past week I've been told my tan is too dark, my hair is too light, I don't dress right for my type, I should open the act singing, and my delivery is better than my material. One of them even went so far as to take a bus to my pad and give me a critical analysis, a free speech lesson and, on departing, borrowed a dime to get back home. I wonder if people tell Lassie he's panting too much or tell Marilyn she's licking her lips too often or say Laughton's too fat and too English . . . Otherwise, I love this Hollywood. Clean living here is IMPOSSIBLE!*

My frustration was spewing out, and as soon as the L.A. gig was over I gladly returned to the San Francisco Purple Onion, yet my family situation only deepened the depression. By now, Sherwood was working as a collection agent for an insurance company, which basically amounted to getting 25¢ a week from poor people, and while I'd been earning $125 a week in L.A. our own debts had spiraled out of control. We had a large tire bill, a grocery bill that ran to about $800 because our little neighborhood store never pushed for the money, and, as far more was going out than coming in, we had no choice but to sell the Fremont Drive house. We'd finally hit rock bottom.

With nowhere to call our own, we had to off-load our furniture on family and friends, and we even had to give our sweet little mongrel, Wags, to Mrs. Clean next door. All of us, especially the kids, were heartbroken. Mrs. Clean had never allowed her own children to have a pet, but once that dog moved into her home she went nuts over it. Wags became her baby. Oh my God, he was pampered and groomed *constantly,* which was a way better deal than I'd ever had—while Wags was living it up, I had to hit the road to make a living, accompanied by Sherwood and our two eldest daughters, Sally and Suzanne. At the same time, our youngest kids, Stephanie and Perry, went to live with Sherwood's mother and sister at the tiny apartment they shared on Shaw Boulevard in St. Louis.

Being separated from those little kids was incredibly upsetting, but we were homeless and I was doing everything I could to earn some serious money. The first place that hired me was the Twin Tree Inn on Lovers Lane in Dallas—a very small but exclusive club that catered to the chicest, richest audiences and which served fantastic food, including steaks that were imported from Minnesota. I was one of four people who worked there, along with Carol Burnett, Don Adams, and Portia Nelson, who was a sophisticated performer of light comedy and self-penned songs.

A couple of gay guys owned the Twin Tree Inn: John Calvert, a former university professor who ran the kitchen and sat at the cash register, and Norwood Ballue, a thin, slightly built maître d' in horn-rimmed glasses who made everybody feel like they couldn't get into the place. Norwood had loved me when he'd caught my routine very early on at the Purple Onion, and this had inspired him to open his own venue with a baby grand piano in a little room and book me as the very first act back in 1955. Until then I had never stayed in a hotel, and I remember sitting in the restaurant for two hours trying to figure out how much I should tip for lunch. I knew nothing.

Regardless, I was now being hired for a return engagement that would commence on December 12, 1956, and last through New Year's Eve. Norwood had an eye for lady entertainers, and he and John were also kind enough to put all four of us up in a nice two-bedroom apartment, while wining and dining us at their gorgeous home in a very upscale Dallas neighborhood.

"Phyllis Diller really had those tall Texans in an uproar during her stay there," reported the January 12, 1957, edition of the *San Francisco Chronicle*. "They even named an oil well after her." Rarely given to overstatement (ha!), the same paper then pressed home the point a couple of days later:

> *The millionaires loved her so much, they promised they'd buy movable portions of S.F. and ship them to Dallas if she'd stay. "It seemed such a nuisance," says Miss Diller, "I just came home."*

That same month, *Variety* reviewed one of my Purple Onion performances and asserted that "So long as she sticks to her own material, Phyllis Diller is an adroitly funny, offbeat comedienne in this intimate basement bistro. Best effort is her takeoff on Eartha Kitt's 'Ridiculous' [sic] from what Miss Diller calls 'the old "New Faces."'" In this routine, she bangs the back-stage wall, takes a pratfall trying to climb aboard the piano, and breaks up the joint. Her running gag with the bunch of plastic cherries pinned to her chest is great, too, and she gets off some nice swipes at psychiatry, slick magazines, and culture generally. Somewhere along the line, however, Miss Diller has picked up about eight minutes' worth of 'Hollywood jokes,' and these hurt her, because they are stale. When she eliminates those gags and goes with her own wacky brand of physical eggheadedness, there'll be no stopping her."

Around this time, realizing we were just one step ahead of the truant officer, Sherwood and I decided to place Sally and Suzy with his family in St. Louis before going back on the road. Or, to be more precise, on the *tracks*. You see, another of Sherry's little foibles was that he refused to fly, so having him with me meant that we had to travel around the country by train, carrying our belongings in cardboard boxes because we couldn't even afford proper luggage. Talk about scraping the bottom of the barrel.

I once tricked Fang. I got him on a very long flight to London and we lost an engine. The captain's voice came over the speaker: "This is nothing to be concerned about. It just means we will be one hour late landing at Heathrow." Then we lost another engine and again the captain spoke: "This is a very powerful aircraft. Don't be apprehensive. It just means we'll be two hours late landing in London." Then we lost another engine and Fang said, "Jesus Christ! We lose one more and we'll be up here all night!"

When the children were on their school vacation in the summer of 1957, I had to find somewhere for all six of us to live while I performed a three-month engagement at the Purple Onion. Barry Drew had fixed it so that, every year, I'd appear at the club from June through August and have my kids with me when school was out. Sherwood, however, refused to look for a home, so I searched alone and the first place I found was an old, wooden, pre-earthquake Victorian building on Van Ness that had been divided into apartments. We were on the middle floor, with apartments above and below us, but when our few pieces of furniture were delivered, the landlady wouldn't allow the piano to be brought into our home. She had it placed in the basement, and I eventually gave it to the pianist at the Purple Onion. Bit by bit, I was losing everything—it's a miracle I didn't lose my mind—and we also had to contend with complaints by the other tenants. Peter was visiting from L.A., and the combined sound of him playing the banjo while tapping his foot on the floor and me typing material for my act resulted in our eviction.

Never mind that I spent my days writing, cooking, and cleaning—well, something like that—before working in the club until two o'clock every morning. Sherwood still wouldn't look for somewhere to live, so once more I had to search alone, and again I found a place . . . but oh boy, *what* a place. It was above a ten-cent store on Hyde Street, just one block—and a world away—from swanky Nob Hill. The apartment was crummy, yet it was large. And given the size of our family, this was important—even if I thought it was strange to have a sink in the corner of every room. Only when I was well into my eighties did I realize this dump must have been a stinking whorehouse! At the time I just wondered, "Why is there a sink in every room? Why? *Why?*" Then a couple of years ago, it finally dawned on me. Oh honey, was *I* naive!

One day, when Peter was back in L.A., the four other kids went down to the ocean. The poor little things, this was a rare chance for them to have some fun. However, one of them had left a faucet running back at the apartment (which wasn't difficult, considering how many faucets we had in that place) and it flooded the ten-cent store. The next day, I had to go in and buy everything on that counter—wet and ruined. Then, on another occasion when the kids were at the ocean park, they lost the youngest, seven-year-old Perry, and searched for him everywhere. Finally, distraught because they couldn't find him, they returned on the bus and saw their baby brother wandering the streets. Imagine, that dear little boy with the gorgeous big, brown eyes, having to grow up surrounded mostly by females while his father was Mr. Zero.

Fang is the cheapest man alive. On Christmas Eve, he puts the kids to bed, fires one shot, and tells them Santa committed suicide. On Thanksgiving, we didn't even have a turkey. We had a meatball with a feather in it.

Sherwood was such a piece of work. I can still picture all of the kids packed into the station wagon, along with a bird in a cage, and him refusing to drive to L.A. when I was heading there to play John Walsh's 881 Club. Here was an able-bodied man whose only desire was to jump on me and have real bad sex, while I was expected to support the family, find us somewhere to live, and now even drive all the way to Los Angeles. Throughout these years, my constant prayer was "Give me strength!"

An August 1957 *Hollywood Reporter* review of my show at John Walsh's 881 described me as "technically a standup comedian who works with a few props but mostly depends on a sharp tongue and an agile mind. She discusses the insanities and inanities of some modern advertising and a variety of other subjects that are connected only by her fertile imagination. Miss Diller is a natural bet for the smart clubs . . . although her material could be sharpened by a little editing and perhaps less intimacy with her audience. But she is the kind of performer who is going to develop a fanatic and devoted clientele. She is a new artist of unusual potential."

The word was getting around: I was *hot*, and this was a view shared by numerous club owners who booked me after catching some of my performances. Among them, Herbert Jacoby of the Blue Angel in New York, and Oscar and George Marienthal who ran Mister Kelly's in Chicago.

The Marienthals really knew how to handle a business. They had three rooms: a breakfast room named Brief Encounter, a jazz room where all of the majors played, and Mister Kelly's, which catered to avant-garde comedy and music. Located on Rush Street, in the heart of downtown, this place was full of jazz lovers, many of them students, and as I did much better business there than I was being paid for, Oscar would take me to a jewelry store and buy me beautiful things. I was always a major hit in Chicago, but the same couldn't be said on the East Coast, where I experienced yet another setback.

The Blue Angel was *the* New York place to work, one that was supposed to lead to the big time. Yul Brynner had appeared there and so had Pearl Bailey and many, many other future stars, yet this East Side venue was nicknamed the "Baby Coffin." For one thing, it's very hard to work anywhere that has the word "blue" in the title, and for another, it was the worst-shaped room that anybody could ever want to perform in unless they were a musician. For a comic it was extremely difficult. On entering, there was a very large and active gay bar where Bobby Short would be playing the piano. Then you walked into this elongated, coffin-like room with a regular stage at one end facing tables the size of thumbtacks. About 225 people would be jammed in there on a good night.

The venues where I worked—Mister Kelly's, the Blue Angel, the Purple Onion, and, later on, the hungry i, the Bon Soir in New York, and the Crescendo in L.A.—were known as "discovery clubs" and they always had a gay bar. It was a circuit, the gays had a great sense of humor, and they also liked our exaggerated personas. They liked Judy Garland, they liked me, they liked Joan Rivers—we were the kind of women they wanted to be. They wanted to be onstage, they wanted to be entertainers, and they wanted to be funny. However, when I first worked at the Blue Angel, in January 1958, they evidently didn't want to *see* me.

I started off at the top of a bill that included Shelley Berman, and my accompanist was Bart Howard, who wrote "Fly Me to the Moon," but my delivery didn't work in that room. It was West Coast and it was much slower than that of the fast-talking East Coast borscht-belt types, so I struggled. There were nights when I bombed and there were many nights when business was lousy, but I always went out and did my best. In fact, I remember an occasion when I was playing another New York club, One Fifth Avenue, and at closing time a party of four came in and said, "We'll give you twenty dollars if you'll do the show." I couldn't do my act to an audience of four people, but in this case I tried . . . for free. I wasn't about to take their money.

Bart Howard wanted to help me, Herbert Jacoby wanted to help me, but everybody had a different idea as to what I should be doing, and they were all wrong. I had to find my own way. Bart's help was very old-fashioned, suggesting music with funny asides, whereas the new thing was to just talk. What's more, his dog bit me. It was a big black standard poodle and that curly sonofabitch hated me on sight . . . or maybe on smell.

So, there I was, getting it from all sides and going home at night to a miserable, miserable room in Hell's Kitchen, on Eighth Avenue, right across the street from the old Madison Square Garden. It was probably the cheapest place in New York, with barely enough space to walk around twin beds, as well as a little closet and a refrigerator on the floor that had to have its door left open so that the contents didn't freeze. Every day at four o'clock, in the next room, some guy would come home from work and beat up his wife. The sounds were horrendous, while out in the linoleum-floored lobby a big, fat, frumpy old woman would sit there with an open Bible on her lap. I was surrounded by madness.

I never realized it back then, but as useless as he was, Sherwood served a purpose in this kind of environment: he was a body and he was male. Women aren't safe running around on their own at night, and so it was a good thing for me to have a man by my side. He went to every show, and oh God, he *loved* it—smoking, drinking beer, and having a wonderful time. He enjoyed the nightclub atmosphere, he enjoyed the association with me, and he enjoyed telling everybody he was Fang. All day long, he would do coffee and cigarettes, and then all night long, it was beer and cigarettes. In that respect, he was real easy to please, even if he made my own life extremely difficult.

Thanks to Sherry's insistence on traveling everywhere by train, our arrival at Pennsylvania Station on our very first trip to New York was an embarrassment. Everyone could hear the pots and pans rattling inside our cardboard-box luggage, and when he tried to hail a cab, the driver refused us service. It just so happened that a cab company inspector overheard this, and, after handing the guy a citation, he then ordered him to take us to our digs in Hell's Kitchen. So it was that my New York nightmare began before I had even opened at the Blue Angel.

I was there for two months and within a few weeks I was no longer top of the bill. Desperate to figure out where I was going wrong, I'd look at my outfit on many, many occasions and think, "Maybe I should give this a face-lift." It was painful. My act wasn't working and I knew it, but I was helpless, paralyzed. Shelley Berman had a record out, and one time when he was about to follow me onstage he asked, "How's the audience?"

"Great," I told him. "Real responsive."

"Terrific," he muttered, looking away, "then they won't like *me*."

You see what he was saying? Apparently, he was highbrow and I was lowbrow. Those comments hurt, but I'd never give in to meanness or negativity. Even when drunken hecklers would shout out things like "Go home," I would blank them out and envision myself as an internationally famous comic. That was quite a far-flung goal for a woman in those days. But then, I was quite a far-flung woman. I believed in me, and although I didn't yet know it, all of my dreams were about to come true.

Six

LIKE AN EXECUTION
WITHOUT THE
BLINDFOLD

Everything is funny as long as it is happening to somebody
else.

— WILL ROGERS

I was determined to take another stab at television, and while
I was in New York during the first few months of 1958 I
became close friends with Tom O'Malley, the booker for
The Jack Paar Show.

Broadcast on NBC five nights a week, this mixture of interviews, sketches, and guest turns had huge ratings and was an
ideal forum for my kind of humor, yet O'Malley refused to book
me because, in his opinion, my material just wasn't right. To me
this was plain ridiculous, not least because standups like Buddy
Hackett and Joey Bishop were semiregulars on the show. So, I
had my pianist, Harold Fonville—who was also a booker—call

the show every day until they finally couldn't take it anymore: "Okay, bring her in." It was a case of anything to stop the calls. As soon as I received the invitation I went to the *Tonight Show* office and performed a number, and that evening I was on the air. That's all it took. One minute my material wasn't right, the next it was perfect.

If I say so myself, I made a sensational appearance on the show, doing my way-out material while stripping from my dress down to my black leotard so that I could perform "Ridiculous." In the middle of my strip, I pulled on a chunk of short green hair (courtesy of the beauty parlor at department store J. Magnin) and said, "This isn't hair, these are nerve ends," and that was the line that got Paar. It just blew him away. The striptease took about three minutes and so did the song. And when it ended, *time stood still*. All of the people onstage and in the audience were seemingly in shock, and there was a moment when nothing happened before the whole place exploded. I knew it, everybody knew it: This was important; this was a happening.

The actor Hans Conried and actress Peggy Cass had already come on before me and they were sitting with Jack. I didn't join them. I just did my thing and went backstage, high on the knowledge that I'd made an enormous impact. Without a doubt, it was *The Jack Paar Show* that put me on the road to success. It was a huge turning point. Jack was crazy about me, and my whole life would be very different if he hadn't fallen in love with me right then and there. I immediately became the golden-haired girl, appearing on his show every few weeks, and it was this exposure that made me commercial, enabling me to go anywhere in the country and fill a room.

Dear Mr. Paar and associates:

Just another viewer speaking, to acclaim the appearance of Phyllis Diller on your program as SENSATIONAL. Would like to see more of her. I have never written a "fan" letter before. Just never had the time, but this young lady has such superb timing and fine sense of the ridiculous, I had to write.

Carl E. Walquist, Jr.

Los Angeles, California

The green hair didn't last long, for by now my image was 1929 chic: the short Chanel evening suit, the blond flapper hairdo known as the Jeanmaire because of the style sported by French ballerina Renée Jeanmaire, and the long cigarette holder. That cigarette holder enabled me to get attention by raising my right hand, just as you would when flagging a cab or trying to speak, and it also provided me with another means of showing mock hostility. I'd flick the ashes, and to this day people swear they saw them fall. The cigarette, however, was solid wood. I've never smoked. That's called illusion, that's called acting, and I'm proud of it. I used that holder to stuff the turkey, I used it as eyebrow tweezers, and I used it as chopsticks when I ended up with a fried-rice jabot. Material like this had never been seen or heard before, but I made the audiences come along with me. I was challenging them to understand it, and if they didn't, then at least their mouths would hang open.

When I started out I was not a standup. I was just another funny gal doing funny things and whatever else came to mind. Oh Christ, I played the piano, I jumped on top of the piano, I played the saxophone, and finally it got down to where I simply had a bunch of props and I couldn't say a funny word without putting on the glasses or the feather boa or the chapeau or the shawl. Well, that was no good. I was still using props on *The Jack Paar Show*, and it was only after I'd make enough appearances and enjoy widespread recognition that I would have the guts to get rid of them.

Nothing that I did was in-your-face. It was all very delicate. I had a lovely soprano lyric voice, and so there was one whole routine where I was a concert diva, starting out with a few bars of German lieder, a little opera, before ending up sloppy as hell with the encores, singing things like "Go Down, Moses." All along there were laughs, but I soon found that I wanted more laughs and so I'd eventually drop the music altogether. My goal was to get laughs—or "boffs"—as close together as possible, and you achieve that by talking, not singing. Boffs were the bottom line.

There had been women standup comics before me: brassy chicks like Belle Barth and Rusty Warren, who turned the air blue with their crude jokes in after-hours hangouts, as well as the far more sophisticated and attractive Jean Carroll, who specialized in witty one-liners about her husband and her home life. Carroll actually made several appearances on *The Ed Sullivan Show*, yet neither she nor any of the other women broke through

on the scale that I did during the late fifties and early sixties—
Jean didn't travel to build a mass audience, and Barth and War-
ren were far too X-rated for television. So, for the first ten years,
I had it all to myself.

Then again, there weren't even many male singles. Most of
them were working in pairs: Martin & Lewis, Allen & Rossi,
Burns & Carlin—standups weren't all that popular at the time,
those like Benny and Hope had moved on to other things, and it
was a wide-open field. I sort of snuck in and no one realized what
I was doing. My material resonated with housewives everywhere.

*Our house is full of bugs. I couldn't care less. I wear flea collars
around both ankles. There isn't a person in our family who's got
the guts to eat raisin toast. . . . I do dinner in three phases:
serve the food, clear the table, bury the dead. . . . One night for
dinner, I fixed something so bad, the cat covered it. . . .*

This stuff was offbeat but women could relate to it, and I also
gave the guys plenty to laugh at. I've always had a very personal
association with the audience, and to this day those people all
feel like they know me—I'm the girl next door, I'm the woman
next door, I'm their Aunt Margaret.

Dear Miss Diller:

We have just returned from San Francisco, the Purple
Onion and You . . . Never have we witnessed such a perfectly timed and presented show . . . We waited in line for
about 15 minutes . . . Someone in the line asked what you

did and our answer was "She just talks, but oh how she talks . . ." Your comments on the "new bride" reminded me of my first experience cooking for a husband . . . Your comments about dressing a chicken made me think of another thing that has happened to me and others of my friends . . . I feel as if I should be writing this with purple ink on onion skin, but shall instead vow to serve nothing but purple onions in our house from this day forward . . .

(Mrs.) Patricia Elsberry

San Jose, California

In retrospect, things often worked out better for me when I let them play out slowly. I mean, never mind the props—for years, many people who knew me thought I'd do a whole lot better if I got rid of Sherry, yet it had been his idea for me to become a comic. The problem was, as my career progressed, I grew more and more frustrated with his unbearable antics.

The fake heart attacks became a regular occurrence, and I eventually couldn't tolerate them anymore because I knew they were designed to control me. One time, when Sherwood was scheduled to have a cardiogram back in St. Louis, his mother, sister, and a few of our kids traveled with us in Jeane's battered old car to visit the heart doctor. On arriving there, however, my husband wouldn't go through the door of the building, and when he got back into the car with Maude and Jeane, I started to cry. You see, he didn't want to have his bluff called. It was another anxiety attack brought on by an all-consuming fear, yet he was as strong as an ox!

By this time, around the middle of 1958, our kids were living among cockroaches because the Dillers were evidently too good to clean their place. I saw cockroaches inside tin cans and boxes of cereal, and if a cockroach dropped onto the table while we were eating, Jeane would just knock it away with her hand. Even their horrible fat Scottie dog was allowed to lift his leg and piss in the kitchen. Still, we left our children there because it was better than putting them in a foster home—the Dillers weren't cruel and they did their best. This was their best. They enrolled the girls in modeling school, and they saved Perry's life by having him attend a wonderful youth program at a local Baptist church. There he found his niche playing basketball, which was a much needed escape for a kid who'd spent much of his life surrounded by women and a sick dad.

The Dillers' home was the right place for our children, it just wasn't ideal. Their teenie little apartment housed Dr. Jeane's treatment room where nobody ever got treated—it would have made sense to convert it back into a bedroom, but then sense never figured into anything that family did. I mean, if the press ever turned up there to interview me, Jeane would try to get her mother into the photos. She obviously thought the great Maude Anderson Diller was responsible for my success. I'll never forget the time a photographer moved some furniture and revealed dust balls the size of bales of hay. It was so embarrassing. Now here I was, outside the medical building, putting up with Sherwood's usual crap, and for once I threw a fit. When I cried, that finally got him through the door. His folks turned to him and said,

"Come on, Sherry, you can do it. Just put one foot in front of the other," and they managed to get him up to the doctor's office.

On another occasion when my worse half went for an examination, the doctor refused to go through with it because Sherry was in a state of such high angst. That's what this man was really suffering from, and it all stemmed from his attitude. He was the king. Nobody could tell him anything. When I look back, I'm amazed that I was able to push forward with my career while I had this albatross around my neck. Worse than no help, he was enough to drive anybody wild.

With some of the money I was earning he bought himself a movie camera, and whenever we traveled by train he would stand in the open car at the end of the carriage and film the railway tracks. That's all we ever had on film: miles and miles of tracks. *Oh, brother.* Again it was just an act, put on to impress a few train passengers. Mr. Big wanted them to think he was making a movie—*who the hell cared?*

Sherry always had to have the big new thing, so when I began wearing contact lenses, he wanted them, too. However, after going for a fitting he never returned to collect them. Of course, I was footing the bill, and those lenses were expensive, but I just couldn't get him to pick them up. I thought, "Jesus, there's another three hundred and fifty bucks down the drain!"

Since I hate confrontation, he was never hounded, never pushed, and we'd never scream or argue. Instead, I'd do whatever it took to keep the peace. Sure, he was making my life absolutely wretched, but his own life couldn't have been happy because he was in real pain, a nervous wreck, completely unable to operate.

The fact that I could go onstage every night and be the life of the party was sheer professionalism. And I was also able to derive comedy out of the misery at home. The funniest things in the world are based in tragedy. That's where comedy comes from.

My family and friends have convinced me to give up cooking altogether. It got so bad, they couldn't lift the garbage. . . . Fang is a wonderful cook. He serves food that melts in your mouth— it's frozen.

The Purple Onion's Barry Drew loved me and I loved him, and he was aware of all my problems. He had a predilection for black men, and one year when I stayed with him on his Sausalito houseboat, we'd drive home from the Onion every night and case the Fillmore district for black guys. Now, after Sherwood and I had moved out of that former whorehouse on Hyde Street, Barry provided us with somewhere to live. One place was around the corner on Green Street, and during my Onion engagement in 1959, he'd even loan us his houseboat and find somewhere else for himself. That's the kind of love I received and which I'll never forget.

Overall, I had done pretty well on my own during those first three-and-a-half years, without a manager, without an agent, without anyone. The owners of the little discovery clubs had seen me and hired me, and they had also talked to one another. Many of them liked me and everything was going really well in terms of bookings, even if my earnings were still pretty modest. The one agent with whom I did work during this period was

Irwin Arthur, who would call me at the Purple Onion to tell me about a job after I'd just finished a gig at two in the morning. Evidently he knew my schedule, and he came through on a freelance basis time and again. But then I signed with a big agency and initially this turned out to be a big mistake.

The General Artists Corporation had tried to place me on their books once before. I'd gone to the company's New York office and had sat down with a young hotshot who didn't impress me at all, making a big show of talking to people on the phone. I had seen right through him and thought, "Bullshit." I didn't like his attitude and I didn't want him as an agent, so I'd left without signing. Now, however, having seen more of my shows and observed how my popularity was continuing to grow, GAC made another attempt to sign me, and this time the agent was a man named Leonard Romm.

Leonard was an agent from way back: an old bald guy with a lot of sharp pencils. The first thing he did when he arrived at work every morning was sharpen those pencils, and he knew a thing or two about selling. As a youth, he had worked in his father's haberdashery where the deal was "If anyone comes in here, you've got to at least sell him a hat." I loved Leonard, so I signed with GAC, although there was no contract. It was all done on a handshake and he was my man. However, we got off to a rocky start.

In the corporate sense, agencies like GAC don't care about anything but the money. When they see you making plenty of dollars, they think you're a success; but that has nothing to do with building a career. Consequently, with the whole world to book, GAC booked me into its own kind of places and these were a disaster. The first was the Fontainebleau Hotel in Miami, where, you might recall, I was fired after just one show thanks to microphone trouble and a long gown that gave the impression I was trying to look attractive. Who would fall for that? It was a really dumb move, instigated by a clueless attempt to connect with an unfamiliar audience.

Although my looks caused me a lot of personal anguish, they were invaluable to my career. In fact, I pity any pretty woman who is starting out as a standup comic. In my case, I had this shmoo nose, the worst possible hairdo for my face—a smooth flapper cut instead of some much-needed height—and virtually no makeup. I knew nothing about it and wouldn't let anybody touch me. It was the witch look, and I'd get cast as a witch both by audiences and by movie directors. It would be my fortune.

Every element had to be in place for my routine to work, everything had to be just right. You see, my figure was okay, but to enhance the onstage effect I'd normally wear short dresses or skirts that exposed my legs. It was my awkward stance that made them look funny, and that stance was nowhere to be seen during my first show at the Fontainebleau. It reappeared during the second show when I reverted to my then-trademark Chanel suit, but by then, of course, the hotel's owner wasn't around to witness the far more enthusiastic audience reaction. He'd already made up his mind. Before I knew it, I was on a plane bound for New York and a future rendered blank by a present without bookings, income, home, or any realistic hope. The dreams and aspirations had been shattered, the career momentum had ground to a halt. I felt desperate.

Having sent the in-laws most of my earnings so that they could care for the children, I was now living with Sherwood at the Hotel Earle on Waverly Place in Greenwich Village. This, like our former Hell's Kitchen "residence," was another joint with a linoleum lobby, costing $60 a week for one room with a mattress as thin as lace, as well as a little unit in the corner with a hot plate and refrigerator but no running water. That meant I had to use the sink in the john to wash the dishes. The Earle was inhabited by people who were either on the way up or on the way down, and its electrical circuitry was so old that, when we first stayed there, everything I plugged in just blew up. To this day, I always associate linoleum lobbies with old, threadbare, semi-dirty places.

Peter stayed with us for about a week while we were at the Earle. He had graduated with honors from Hollywood High, and as a means of working his way through UCLA he'd been employed nights at a supermarket, sweeping away the cockroaches. Not too surprisingly, he couldn't take that for long, so after deciding that he needed a complete change of scenery he relocated to New York and slept on the couch in our room just to get his bearings. Next, he got a job at the Lamport fabric house on Seventh Avenue, where he'd work steadily for the next three years, while living in some horrible places and suffering through very rough times in an awfully big city. Extremely frugal, he began saving every cent for his college tuition, but even then Sherwood and I were so broke that we had to borrow about three hundred bucks from him! Thank God that, by the time he did make it to Washington University in St. Louis, I'd be in a position to pay his tuition.

Fang was in a wretched mood. He was doing push-ups in the nude and he didn't notice the mousetrap. . . . He's so cheap, he threw an IOU into a wishing well. I tossed in a dime, and he jumped in after it and broke his neck. That was my wish.

A hot banjo player, Peter played with Laurie Brewis in the Earle's bar, the Waverly Lounge, every Saturday and Sunday, even after we left. Laurie was the pianist in this crummy hotel, and yet he was so good that he was listed in *The New Yorker* magazine. He knew every show tune from the earliest to the most contemporary, and as he was gay and also very good friends with us he would protect Peter from any guys who might hit on him. Peter sat in with all of these terrific musicians in the Village. They'd get together once a week and play Dixieland jazz for fun, and Peter got along swell with them. This was really important at a formative juncture in his life.

In the meantime, I had a female manager, and she was yet another big mistake. Her name was Mary Kelly, she had booked the *Today* show on TV, and when you're a booker everyone's kissing your ass. Well, she mistook that for true love. She was a rough-talking lesbian who had signed six people to managerial contracts before I came along, but what I didn't know was that they had already left her. This was probably due to the fact that she didn't do a thing except make enemies—standing in her little office one day, I heard her tell someone on the phone, "Go fuck yourself." For me this was the final straw. I fired her. Still, it was Mary who had accompanied me to the Fontainebleau while Sherwood remained in the Village, and I returned to New York the morning after the engagement was terminated. From the Fontainebleau to the Earle within just a few torturous hours—what a trip.

At the time I cried, but in retrospect that horrible failure was actually the greatest thing that ever happened to me. It meant that I was in New York for a couple of weeks, and although I spent a fair amount of time stewing in my room, Jack Paar also used me because I was around—I was so hot on his shows that they all became reruns. Jack was absolutely wild about me and he even hired me as a writer, so returning from Miami and spending a fortnight in New York was perfect timing.

As for the Fontainebleau, I'd return there when I was a big star, and I'd also work at other major Miami Beach hotels such as the Deauville and the Eden Roc. Things just weren't right when I was first thrown in there, like some sort of chic gladiator to the lions. Frightened out of my wits in the long dress, and contending with mic trouble and an owner who never bothered to see the second show, I didn't stand a chance. And I also didn't fare much better when I was scheduled to make my debut on NBC's *Steve Allen Show,* which went head-to-head on Sunday nights with *Ed Sullivan.*

I was supposed to appear in a skit about a poltergeist, and I turned up for three rehearsals, but when the people in the deli where I shopped on Eighth Street asked how it was going, I broke down and sobbed. You see, I'd just been fired. One of Steve's writers was Leonard Stern, a tall, dark guy with a beard who had also written for *The Honeymooners* and *The Phil Silvers Show*, and for some reason that guy hated my guts. He was always around when I failed. Doesn't that tell you something? At one TV audition, he didn't even open his eyes. Fortunately, I'd end up making a load of appearances with Steve Allen—everything went fine as long as that guy with the beard wasn't around.

It was towards the end of 1958 that things began to turn around. My act came together as I perfected the crazed housewife persona, and my stock rose in line with more *Jack Paar Show* appearances. Among the admirers was my longtime idol, Bob Hope, who saw me on the tube and then went out of his way to catch one of my shows on the road. The only problem was, this was hardly in the kind of setting that I would have chosen for our first encounter.

Making what appeared to be a compete U-turn from the Fontainebleau, GAC had booked me into an awful little hole in Washington, D.C., called the Lotus Club. This was located within a basement Chinese restaurant that was supposedly a hotspot for top entertainment—Liberace had just played there and his sequins were still in the dressing room. I was on a bill with the Irish Senorita, who sang and wore white duck pants, as well as an opening act consisting of six girls who were expected to mingle. This should tell you something about the kind of audience I was supposed to entertain: salesmen and hookers. There was no way. Every night felt like an execution without the blindfold.

On the evening that Bob came in I tried to sneak out after

my bit, but he jumped up and stopped me: "Phyllis, you're sensational."

"Oh, dear. You just saw me bomb."

"Yeah, but I've seen you quite a few times on the Paar show, and you're great."

"Wow, *thank you.* You don't know what this means to me."

I *absolutely* knew what he meant when he said I was great. My material was great, my delivery was great, I even handled bombing great, and all the while I remained a lady in the eyes of the audience. That isn't easy for a female comic. Out of the blue, in that sleazy sweatbox, I'd heard the kinds of words that made it all worthwhile. Bob wasn't about to hire me—he'd wait until I was his equal in terms of what I could do as a standup—but I said to myself, "If Bob Hope likes my work, I must have *something.*"

GAC's Leonard Romm was thinking along similar lines. He was very, very protective of me, and, after ensuring that the idiotic bookings stopped, it was Leonard who would soon be placing me in way better joints than that god-awful Lotus Club. One such place was the Bon Soir on Eighth Street in Greenwich Village, yet another dingy basement club with the inevitable gay bar, where the small, shaded bulb over the cash register provided much of the light in an all-black room. The Bon Soir attracted chic audiences, and they were far more in tune with my material as well as my laid-back, West Coast delivery.

Isn't my fur stole pitiful? How unsuccessful can a girl look? People think I'm wearing anchovies. The worst of it is, I trapped these under my own sink.

142

On any given night, after emerging from a minuscule dressing room that boasted hooks on the wall to hang my clothes and an air-conditioning unit that dripped water into a bucket, I would look out into the packed audience and see John Gielgud, Marlene Dietrich, Tallulah Bankhead, Ricardo Montalban, Red Buttons, or Broadway columnist Dorothy Kilgallen with her lover, Johnny Ray. The place was a star trap as well as a rat trap, and during my act I'd refer to it as "this cesspool of culture," while pointing out that "the lumps in the rug have been here a long time, and some of them are people."

Dorothy Kilgallen was actually married to the radio actor and producer Dick Kollmar, who owned a little East Side jazz club called the Left Bank. He came to the Bon Soir, fell in love with me and my act, and booked me into his club. This consisted of a badly shaped room that was okay for jazz but not so great for standup. It was wide with hardly any depth, and the "stage" was in the center of the long rear wall. The place didn't even have a dressing room—jazz people don't change their clothes—so I had to go outside and upstairs to an office in order to change. Well, late one night it was snowing, and during my show there were just five people in a booth positioned directly in front of me. All I was doing was talking, and one guy had passed out and his head was on the table. The other four people were so embarrassed that they couldn't laugh, and there I was, going on with my act. At this point I was still green, I was no Don Rickles. I couldn't ad-lib my own name. So on and on I went, and that was one of the most murderous experiences of my career. To make it in standup, you need a bucket of guts and a lot of know-how.

Fortunately, it was a different story back at the Bon Soir. Given immediate star billing, I broke all box office records there during my first season in the fall of 'fifty-nine, and when I returned the following year I was on a roll. Still, as good as my recent progress had been, I'd occasionally run into the kind of no-holds-barred talent and ambition that clearly neither luck nor inexperience could restrain for very long. This is what happened in September 1960, when I came face-to-face with a brilliant young singer whose breathtaking voice had earned her a week-long engagement at the Bon Soir, after she'd already won a contest at a nearby gay bar called The Lion. The lady's name was Barbra Streisand.

When Barbra was introduced to me in the Bon Soir's antiquated dressing room, she was dressed from top to bottom in clothing that she had bought at used stores: a wonderful blouse that had belonged to some fabulous woman, a skirt, and a pair of shoes that she told me she adored because she'd paid just 35¢ for them. Years later, when she appeared in *Funny Girl,* the filmmakers would copy all of those secondhand gems. Barbra loved those old clothes and they were perfect for her. She always knew exactly what she was doing and what was just right for her, even as a teenager.

On her opening night at the Bon Soir, Barbra performed just a few numbers, including "Keepin' Out of Mischief Now," "A Sleepin' Bee," "I Want to Be Bad," "When Sunny Gets Blue," and, most magnificent of all, "Who's Afraid of the Big Bad Wolf." During the previous five years I had worked with many young singers who aspired to greatness and they'd all sung melancholy love songs, but now here was this incredible material. "Who's Afraid of the Big Bad Wolf" was an up-tempo tune featuring a fantastic voice, and when I heard it I had an immediate epiphany: "This is a *great* star." The performance just blew me away. By the third tone, honest to God, I had goose pimples and every hair on my body was standing up. She was that sensational.

After that first night, somebody went to the club's manager and reported that she'd overheard a comment in the ladies' room that Barbra was a wonderful singer who dressed horribly. What did any of them know? Barbra was dressed exactly right, but the manager asked me to take her out and buy her something "normal." We therefore spent an entire day shopping, mainly at S. Klein's, the low-priced department store at Fourth Avenue and Union Square, and after Barbra had tried on about a thousand dresses and eighteen hundred pairs of shoes, we finally got her a darling pair of modern high heels and a black chiffon dress. That dress was featured in *Vogue* and *Bazaar*, but she never wore it.

On about the third day, she said, "Phyllis, would you be offended if I returned that dress and used the money to buy some material? Some friends of mine could use it to make me a gown."

"Of course not," I replied. It was clear to me that she knew exactly what to wear and that it shouldn't be off the rack or out of *Vogue*.

Back then, Barbra was contained, reserved, and not at all outgoing. She was a girl who was determined to become a big film star. She didn't want to be a singer. In fact, one night I had to go on in her place because she was watching a movie. She studied movies and she'd go see them all day long, and on that particular night, the film was more important to her than getting to work on time. That really didn't bother me, but what I did do was lecture her right away about her nose, a subject that I knew all about.

I said, "I've been around the block and I've dealt with agents, and I know what is going to happen to you. Every agent is going to tell you that you have to have a nose job. Don't ever, ever do it." Of course, I gave her a couple of days to get to know me before imparting such solid advice. I knew those cheap assholes would go straight for her nose, and they did, but by then I had already girded her loins . . . or, as they say in New York, *goided her lerns*. Sure, my nose was a broken mess, but no agents ever asked me to fix it. I was a comic, so they didn't want me to be pretty. Singers are meant to be beautiful. However, just like her voice, Barbra's nose fit her face. It's her shining glory. She *is* that nose.

My self-confidence was growing along with my stature on the showbiz scene. I was a hot ticket at the Bon Soir, and soon venues across the country, from Minneapolis, Minnesota, to Hot Springs, Arkansas, would be willing to shell out the kinds of fees that I could have only dreamed about a short time earlier. My final three-month summer engagement at the Purple Onion had earned me a massive $2,000 a week, and the club didn't even have a problem when I subsequently accepted an offer to make $3,000 a week at the hungry i. You see, it reaps dividends when you're a good person who really works for a place instead of behaving like a big star with big demands. And I was now also such a well-known part of the North Beach scene that, thanks to word of mouth, many of the tourists who came to town were pointed in the direction of both venues.

As I had learned at the start of this whole process, there truly is a magic of believing. And now, having worked my way to the top of the discovery club circuit, I was already making the moves that were about to transform my life and shift everything into a much higher gear.

Seven

THE TRUTH
ABOUT FANG

1 960 was some year for me, a year of exhilarating and fascinating changes preceding the dawn of the Kennedy era,
when a combination of hope and uncertainty would mirror
my own professional and domestic circumstances. Having previously flunked a screen test directed by Jerry Lewis at Paramount,
I could thank Leonard Romm, my fabulous agent at GAC, for
landing me the cameo role of flamboyant actress, singer, and speak-
easy proprietor Texas Guinan in *Splendor in the Grass*.

A real-life character within this fictional story about a pair of
confused and tormented young would-be lovers in 1920s Kansas,
Texas was a brassy, no-nonsense Jazz Age dame who wore glitzy

clothes, had a dyed-blond flapper hairdo, and traded good-natured barbs with her audiences after greeting them with her trademark, "Hello, suckers! Come on in and leave your wallet on the bar." It was a tiny role that suited me down to the ground.

Filmed in New York City, and costarring Warren Beatty and Natalie Wood as the troubled adolescents, this movie was directed by Elia Kazan, featured an Oscar-winning screenplay by William Inge, and was a complete departure from anything I'd ever done. I *loved* it. The nightclub scene in which I was involved took a couple of days to shoot and utilized two hundred extras, and in the course of trying to get a performance out of me Kazan said, "Think of someone you *hate*." For years I had worked really hard to discard any feelings of hate and just love everybody—love was the key—so his directive left me completely blank. (Boy, could I respond differently now.) Then, in the middle of helming this big scene, he said, "Strike the take for a mo," and I thought, "What language is this?" Oh honey, even if I wasn't young, I was still tender and naive.

I met my idol, Warren Beatty. I was so thrilled, and he was thrilled, too . . . He finally met a woman he didn't want.

Next, that summer I made my dramatic stage debut as Lottie Lacey, the second lead in *The Dark at the Top of the Stairs,* which focused on the trials, tribulations, and inner demons of a dysfunctional family in 1920s Oklahoma. Again written by William Inge, and performed under the direction of William Hunt at three Long Island venues—the North Shore Playhouse in Bayville,

the Marymede Playhouse in Smithtown, and the Red Barn Theatre in Northport—the play had been turned into a movie just a
few months earlier, with Eve Arden playing Lottie.

In November, I then made my first appearance on *The Ed Sullivan Show*, CBS TV's Sunday night institution that was capable
of juxtaposing comics, chorus girls, and jugglers with grand opera,
ballet, and scenes from a current Broadway hit. This meant max-
imum exposure in front of a nationwide audience, yet I had always known I would never get on *Sullivan* with props, and I'll
never forget the first night I walked onto a stage without them.
Normally, I would stand in the crook of the piano and the props
would be in a box beside me, but now they weren't there and the
floor manager couldn't believe it. He said, "What, you've got no
props?" For me this was a big step and it was very difficult, because I'd have to be funny without the glasses, without the hat,
without the shawl. Props are just that: they're a crutch, and you're
never going to the top with a prop. (Hey, that's a *good line*.) So,
having noticed that all of the standup comics I had ever seen—
singles like Shecky Greene and Alan King—stood alone in front
of the curtain, I forced myself to do the same and before long I
was on the *Sullivan* show.

The old guy who booked Ed's overseas acts was mad about me
and determined to get me on the show. I wasn't his responsibility, but he secured me a private audition with Ed Sullivan in his
six-room, eleventh-floor apartment suite at the Hotel Delmonico
on New York's Park Avenue. I went up there one morning and it
was real uncomfortable. Here was Ed in his dressing robe and
slippers, coughing while I ran through my act in his living room

and his dog sniffed my toes. That little bastard. How can you concentrate when a dog is sniffing your toes and Ed Sullivan is sitting in a robe, coughing? Needless to say, he didn't crack a smile. He simply looked bothered and abused, wishing he was asleep this early in the morning. It was probably the only private audition he'd ever given, and although he never said a word of encouragement—not even a "Thank you, we'll be in touch"—I was on his show a short time later.

Everything that goes wrong is my husband's fault. Last night he put the car in the garage backwards. Well, that shot the heck out of my map. This morning I drove out the wrong end, going the wrong way on a one-way street. When I finally got home, you should have seen Fang. He wanted to know how I had driven into the kitchen. I'd made a left turn from the dining room, of course!

A spot on *Sullivan* was a big deal. Yet, just over a decade later, following numerous appearances, I actually pulled out of his final show. Terribly rushed and far too busy, I didn't get my material on cue-cards early enough. For some strange reason the cue-card man was making mine within sight of Ed, who knew *nothing* about comedy, and as Ed read them he began removing all the jokes, leaving just the setup lines. That was too much. Even though I'd been advertised to appear, I walked, and afterwards I received an apology from Ed's son-in-law who produced and directed the show. Don't forget, Ed Sullivan was the guy who came out on

New Year's Eve and said, "Happy Thanksgiving!" He was Mr. Malaprop.

I, meanwhile, was always working with new material and always trying to remember what I was going to say. I had to have at least five minutes of absolute silence, with nobody around, in order to just screw my head on beforehand. You might call it meditation or self-hypnotism, but I had to pull myself together and that took a great effort. I can ad-lib and I'm good at it, but during the early sixties I didn't do that. And I also rarely used cue cards, even though I did once go blank . . . on *live television*. For a second, I couldn't get the words out: "A-fa-fa-la-cha-ca-ca-fa-ca-pa-ja-ca . . ." *Blank!* What could I do? I went to some bit I remembered, which wasn't where I was supposed to go, but at least I kept talking and no one ever knew. I tell you, for the first ten years, I shook. It was nerve-racking and I was terrified, yet there was a tremendous upside to all this work.

Performing at the Bon Soir in New York, I would meet many of the celebrities who came to watch my show, and one night Sherwood and I were invited by Tallulah Bankhead to have dinner with her and jazz pianist Joe Bushkin. Tallulah, that legendary actress of the sharp mind, quick wit, and deep, raspy voice, whose penchant for booze sparked an explosive laugh and even more volatile personality—how could I resist? I wasn't a big star, and it was really sweet of her to invite me. So, after somehow persuading Sherry to come along, I visited her East Side town house.

There, on the second floor, was a living room with a fireplace, and nearby was a dish for Dolores, the white Maltese poodle that

Joe and his wife had bought for Tallulah . . . and which she had once accidentally set on fire. Introducing us to Dolores while deliberating over her own pills, Tallulah asserted that the dog had belonged to Saint Paul—from the start this was clearly going to be a *different* kind of evening. Tallulah was wearing a peignoir with nothing underneath, and she kept throwing it up into the air while we ate a dinner that consisted of Southern fried chicken. Then Joe left to do a show at the Basin Street East, and Sherwood and I remained behind for drinks before accompanying our hostess up to her bedroom. It was quite a place, with cigarette burns all over the bedding—I remember counting eighty-three. Still, here was the wonderful old Tallulah in her favorite domain, slurring her words while making grand, sweeping hand gestures, and I'm *sure* she had a crush on me. Sherry didn't notice. But then, he rarely did.

In the summer of 1961, shortly after my long-awaited debut at San Francisco's hungry i, Sally started accompanying me on the road so that, according to newspaper reports, she could "get an inside look at the showbiz world." Nothing could have been further from the truth. The fact was, at the age of seventeen my oldest daughter was spiraling out of control, her behavior becoming increasingly strange and erratic, and this was my latest, desperate attempt to turn things around: to avoid the conclusion that she was an incurable schizophrenic who had to be institutionalized.

Silly me, for years I kept fooling myself that she would get well, but even though I did everything I could for her, nothing was ever enough. One time she wanted a nose job, so I got her the nose job. But then she said, "Now I'd like my jaw fixed," and

I thought, "Oh, my God, what have I started?" I would lean over backwards, do anything for peace, but it was clear that nothing could make Sally happy. She was at odds with herself, at odds with the world, and all the while I had to contend with her problems on my own because Sherwood was no help at all. He was just there.

We named all our children Kid. Well, they have different first names, like Hey Kid, You Kid, Dumb Kid . . . And they are dumb. But Fang is even dumber. He thinks he's their father . . . One of them asked him to spell Mississippi. He said, "The river or the state?"

By early 1962, thanks to my now earning several thousand dollars a week, we were no longer rotting away inside a room at the Earle, but living in a suite at the Waldorf-Astoria in New York City. Of course, the Waldorf was Sherwood's idea—it filled him with the sense of importance to which he felt entitled. And although I'm not saying I didn't like it there, we would have been better off in a hotel where more show people stayed. Regardless, it was in New York on May 25 that I played Carnegie Hall with a show titled *Just Phyllis Diller*. This was a definite high point at a time when I was on a roll: Carnegie, the Seattle World's Fair . . . if there was a great booking, I got it. God, I was as hot as a pistol, although I had no idea I was so hot. I just took everything in my stride. The magic was working and nothing surprised me. And the public also had no clue as to what was going on behind the scenes.

One opening night, in our suite at the Waldorf, Sherwood sat in the bedroom fully dressed while several press guys were in the parlor. They all knew my husband was in town, and when he didn't appear, they kept asking, "Where's Fang?" What could I say? "He's all dressed up in the next room but he can't get through the door"? He was always putting me in that position. On another occasion, it was opening night in Las Vegas and I should have been having a ton of fun—it was a *big* deal—but when I showed up at our hotel suite Sherwood greeted me with a tirade. Obviously, he was alone, he was scared, and he was having an anxiety attack, so I came home to just hours and hours of angry talk. He wasn't threatening, but he wouldn't quit. I had to contend with all his pent-up emotion.

Then there was the time I played Vancouver, and Cliff Arquette, who enjoyed brief success as the baggy-pants character Charlie Weaver on *The Jack Paar Show*, wanted me to play a nurse in some TV skit. I had to take a flight to L.A. on my day off, a Sunday, but when I arrived home after doing two shows the night before, Sherwood just wouldn't stop talking. He obviously didn't want me to go, so he kept going on and on and on, and I ended up having to put the pillow over my head in order to get a little sleep. I mean, I was *going* to board that small one-engine plane and I was sure as hell going to be there for the show. The only problem was, after a night of hell listening to my husband's manic ranting, it was some kind of flight—everything was fogged in and this little airplane was navigating its way around mountains. Such fun. Thankfully, it landed okay and I did the show, but then when I returned home he was still talking: *Blah-blah-blah-blah-blah-blah-blah*—pure madness.

Unaware that he was mentally ill, I just thought, *"Shut up!"* He upset me so much, I was a nervous wreck; yet between the anxiety attacks and subconscious jealousy over my career, he was in a terrible state. Here was a guy who was scared to death of being asked, "What do you do for a living?" As far as I was concerned, it was fine if he accompanied me and ensured that I wasn't alone, but all of that demented behavior—*oh, Jesus!* He pretended that he had a lot to do with the business side of my career, and he did make an effort—he'd work for hours on the design and distribution of these cute little pamphlets that listed my show schedules, and he'd also send handwritten notes on scraps of paper to club owners, informing them about my skyrocketing career. However, although he would have liked to think of himself as my manager, he didn't have a clue about what a manager is or does.

On our wedding day, Fang strained his back carrying me over the threshold and he hasn't worked a day since. I call him Samson—even a haircut weakens him! He's still lying on the couch in his wedding suit. I have to lie down on the floor next to that couch to see what he looks like standing up. One time I said, "You should jog around the block." He said, "Why? I'm already here."

Once, when I was performing in Minneapolis and scheduled to appear on *The Ed Sullivan Show*, I had to travel to Chicago overnight on a Saturday so that I could pick up a TWA flight to New York in time for the Sunday afternoon rehearsal and p.m. broadcast. To do this, we hired a teeny little private plane without realizing it was being flown by a couple of teenagers, and when I sat directly behind them in the only other seat, they gave me a stuffed animal because I was their *first passenger* . . . oh, brother. I just sat there, staring at their skinny little necks while the control tower guided these kids all the way to Chicago, and they did a fine job. However, shortly after we arrived I discovered that Sherwood had forgotten to book the flight to New York. Initially, TWA refused to allow me on board and for good reason— the plane was so crowded that luggage was actually strapped into the front row of seats. Yet, I somehow talked my way onto that flight, making a song and dance about my appearance on *Sullivan*. This wasn't the first time that my supposed "manager" had failed to make the necessary arrangements, and it wouldn't be the last.

In the spring of 1962, I paid $20,000 cash for an eleven-room colonial house on Mason Avenue in affluent Webster Groves, just ten miles southwest of St. Louis—the children had lived there so long, it was their home, and this property realized my longtime promise to them that one day they'd each have their own room. It had a pink stucco exterior, white shutters, a pool in the backyard, and classic artwork and antique furniture throughout; yet with a husband and daughter both skidding off the rails, how could I enjoy any of this? Soon after we moved, I walked into Sally's bedroom and discovered her sitting facing the corner with a razorblade in her hand. Up until now, even though I'd always danced around her, she had at least been sweet, but this was a whole other ball game and I knew I was out of my depth. That's when I realized she had to go into an institution. What's more, I'd have to take care of this myself. Sherwood, as usual, wouldn't do a thing. I therefore placed her in the Steinberg psychiatric unit of Barnes, the best hospital in St. Louis, and a short time later I also had to get her out of there when one of the other girls was raped.

I kept putting Sally in different places, halfway houses, always thinking and hoping that something could be done. Medication, therapy sessions, electric shock treatment—it quickly became clear that *nothing* could be done, but as a parent I was in denial. That is until the day came when she was back on the road with me: We were staying in the penthouse suite of the Fairmount Hotel in San Francisco, and she locked the front door and refused to let me in. What if she opened a window? I was in such a state. At that point, she returned to an institution full-time, and although I'd visit her, Sherwood wouldn't so much as write. For him, she no longer existed.

Meanwhile, it was when we moved to Webster Groves that my spouse took on yet another charming habit: refusing to bathe. Don't ask me why. I'd run the water and put the kids' toy boats in there—as usual, I was taking the light approach, the sweet approach, the let's-have-fun approach, but he'd just plain refuse to get into that tub. And when he stayed in St. Louis to take care of Stephanie, Suzy, and Perry, he often wouldn't leave the house. He'd either send for the barber or get one of the kids to cut his hair, and he would also call a taxi and have the driver bring him a six-pack of beer. Then, after he drank that, he would call the cab again and order another six-pack. He didn't have the sense to send for a case. He only knew how to spend my money. I mean, here he was, hiring a gardener to mow a tiny patch of grass in the front yard—again, this was for the neighbors to see.

Fang's idea of a seven-course dinner is a six-pack and a bologna sandwich. The last time I said, "Let's eat out," we ate in the garage. . . . He staggered out of a bar one night, threw up on a cat, and said, "I don't remember eating that." I've done every-thing I know to make that man stop drinking. I threatened him, "If you don't give up this stupid drinking, I am going to cut you off from sex altogether!" He said, "You don't even know where I'm getting it."

Once, when I had tickets to see *My Fair Lady*, we sat for just six minutes before Sherry said he had to leave, made me accom-pany him because I was driving, and then wouldn't let me return. Again, it was a case of anxiety combined with passive aggression. Thank God I still adhered to *The Magic of Believing*. Every Christmas, when I was at my peak, an awful lot of people re-ceived presents from me. In 1961, I had sent each of them a round, grapefruit-sized, white leather-bound notebook from Saks Fifth Avenue, and I'd kept one for myself. This was my "dream book," and for more than forty years, I've made entries as part of an ongoing process. I still have several pages to fill.

The very first entry was a pen drawing of a castle. At the time,

I had no idea why I did this, unaware that I'd soon play Disneyland and Disney World while also marrying someone whose brother would become the head of Disney. Then I drew some cars—I'd been given a brand-new station wagon as part payment for doing a commercial, but Sherwood wouldn't pick it up when I was on the road, so I never actually received it. That's why we didn't have a car when we lived in St. Louis. However, as my dream book illustrated, I wanted lots of them. My love for cars came from my daddy, and I'd end up owning five at the same time.

The next entry stated BEVERLY HILLS, alongside a drawing of a large house, palm trees, and a swimming pool, as well as PENTHOUSE IN NEW YORK, next to a drawing of a high-rise—I'm still living the Beverly Hills lifestyle, and I'd also have an apartment overlooking the East River when starring on Broadway in *Hello, Dolly!* And although a number of entries never came true—most notably Sally getting well—some of my projections were uncanny:

BEST SELLERS—I'd be the author of four best-selling comedy books; a sketch of me on the big screen—I'd make more than twenty-five movies; THE PHYLLIS DILLER SHOW—I'd have three different TV shows; REALLY GREAT SYMPHONIES—I'd eventually perform in these; OFFICE BUILDINGS—I'd part-own one on Sunset Boulevard; OIL WELLS—again, I would part-own some; DOCTORAL DEGREES—I'd be awarded a couple of honorary ones; another money bag, this time with $10 MILLION on it—when I drew this, it really didn't make much sense, but again my dream would come true; LOVE, ENERGY, HEALTH, VOICE, CREATIVITY, MUSIC, COMFORT,

GRACE, EASE, EXPANSION, BEAUTY, ART, FRIENDSHIP, TRAVEL, PRO-
DUCTION, SOBRIETY, VISION, SIGHT, MAGNETISM, MONEY—these
pretty much spoke for themselves. You've gotta make a list, baby!

I didn't chase things. Once I had delineated my dreams, I knew
they would come to me, and these included love. Nothing will
help more to make a man turn and run the other way than sensing you want him. That's why my advice to girls is, be a prize, not
a trap. After all, men are supposedly the aggressors. They want to
chase, so you've got to run . . . or at least crawl. Run but *hesitate*.

It was in the summer of 'sixty-two that I met Warde Donovan
Tatum. Appearing in a Chicago production of the Leonard Bern-
stein musical *Wonderful Town* at the Melody Top Theater—a
huge tent in the southwest suburb of Hillside—I portrayed the
central character of plain-but-practical author Ruth, based on
that of Ruth McKenney who had penned the stories of *My Sister
Eileen* a quarter-century earlier. Ruth was the smart sister while
Eileen was the pretty one. And Warde, who omitted the Tatum
designation from his stage name, played my leading man, editor
Robert Baker, having already portrayed the Wreck opposite
Carol Channing in a Broadway production of the same musical.

> *Miss Diller, who is aggressively homely, transforms the role into
> a combination of Mrs. Kallikak and good old Aunt Maud down
> on the farm who always punctuated her hillbilly humor with a
> "That's what I said, by cracky," wink or elbow nudge. Some-
> times the humor strikes and the laughs come, for Miss Diller is a
> skillful oddball who is often a stitch to watch.*
>
> Chicago Tribune, *July 31, 1962*

Phyllis Diller is not a singer or a musical comedy star. She is a comedienne, a contortionist, and a good sport—and in Wonderful Town, *which opened Monday night at Melody Top, she should surely get a nod for gumption, if not for genius. Eileen never had a sister that could bat an eye or drop a jaw like this one.*
—Chicago Sun-Times, *August 1, 1962*

Warde had worked for eighteen months on the London stage in *Zip Goes a Million*, as well as on Broadway in *Saratoga*, *By the Beautiful Sea*, and *Destry Rides Again*. At one time he even had his own show out of New York, *Warde Donovan Sings*. Well, let me tell you; as soon as I set eyes on him during the first rehearsal of *Wonderful Town* the effect was instant, and within a couple of days the two of us were in the sack. He was tall and handsome with blue eyes, and *very* good at sex. Oh honey, when you've been abused for over twenty years, that really means something. The physical attraction was really, really strong, and I was nuts about him like I'd never been nuts about anyone before. We were both married—and I'd had my one-night stands on the road, which were all accidents—but this was the real thing, baby, with sparks and cannons going off and great physical chemistry.

Warde's big song in the show was "A Quiet Girl," and, boy, did he sing the heck out of it. He had a gorgeous baritone voice and great control, and to me he was a prince when he walked on that stage. I'd watch him from the wings every night, *mesmerized*, and when we were away from the theater he'd kid me by singing, "I love a *gentile* girl." However, he was not a natural performer. There was a certain kind of phoniness to everything he did, and he also suffered from extreme nervousness, so by the time I met him he was very much on the way down, earning just $400 a week.

Although I was normally attracted to guys with brains, in this case I didn't care and I'd eventually come to realize that he was quite dumb. Warde had fallen out of a second-story window when he was two, and I'm sure this had permanently affected him. However, he was six-two with eyes of blue and a voice that just made me crazy, so *come on!* The whole thing was physical, he was physical, and I had never been involved with anyone like that . . . aside from Sherwood, with whom I didn't *want* to be physical.

A fellow went into a drugstore and asked to speak with a male pharmacist, and the lady there said, "My sister and I have owned this store for thirty years, so don't be embarrassed. Just tell us your problem and we'll solve it." He said, "Well, it is embarrassing. I, uh, suffer from continuous sexual arousal." She said, "Don't worry, let me talk to my sister." So they had a conference and she came back and said, "The best we can do is a thousand a week and half of the store."

Once the run of *Wonderful Town* was over, I'd get together with Warde wherever he was performing, he would attend parties at our house in St. Louis, and the following year, we again played summer stock in Chicago, costarring in Anita Loos's *Happy Birthday* at the Drury Lane Theatre. By then, it must have been pretty clear to anyone who knew us that we were madly in love, so Sherwood was more than a little suspicious. He would have done anything to get on an airplane and catch us together. However, since he was scared to fly, I always knew where he was. I'd simply call him at home every day.

One time, I was playing a strange place in the San Fernando Valley called the Palomino Club—it didn't have a dressing room, just an outside trailer—and Sherry called the bar there every night. He would ask the staff to leave the phone open so he could listen to my show *over the phone.* It made absolutely no sense. He still wanted to give the impression that he was managing me, but he couldn't sell Windex to a Peeping Tom.

Looking back, this was an incredible period for me. Here I was, madly in love with one man, putting up with another, and all the while my career was going gangbusters. It was hardly a settled time, but at least it was action-packed—what a difference a decade makes. At the start of the fifties, I had been a bored and abused housewife. Now it was nose to the grindstone, saying yes to everything and never looking to the left or right. I agreed to every interview, every photo opportunity, every benefit show, totally focused on my career and pushing forward all the time. There was no way I could relax in those days. What's more, due to the magic of believing, there was never a thought on my part that the success wouldn't last. I pictured it continuing up until the very end, even if there was still the occasional setback.

In a horrible move reminiscent of my engagement at Miami's Fontainebleau Hotel several years earlier, an agent at GAC booked me into the Copacabana in January 1963 and it was a disaster. For most performers back then, the Copa was *the* feather in the cap—the New York nightclub where greats such as Frank Sinatra and Sammy Davis, Jr., trod the boards. I was signed to play three engagements there at $3,000, $5,000, and $7,000, but after fulfilling the first assignment, I then bailed on the other two. The Copa was not my audience, and it could have ended my career had I tried to stay there—the place was full of rag merchants with hookers who didn't have a home. They wanted rapid-fire jokes and plenty of Copa girls, and I couldn't be a part of that. It was obvious I was in the wrong place, so I had no qualms whatsoever about walking away. I knew how to handle my line of business.

Some time earlier, when Jackie Mason got a shot at the Copa, his representative approached me at the Blue Angel and said, "Jackie wants to try out some new material because he's appearing on *The Jack Paar Show*." You see, he was working at the Copa but he couldn't try out the new material there, so I was being asked if he could test it on my audience. I said he could, and instead of staying in my dressing room, I even came down and watched his act, applauding and doing the whole gracious lady thing. However, Jackie never even bothered to thank me. So much for gratitude. And besides, his act was hardly original.

June 7, 1963, was pronounced "Phyllis Diller Day" in San Francisco by Mayor George Christopher. That afternoon, after being met by an official party at the airport, I was given a motorcade escort into the city, and in the evening, I appeared at the

Masonic Temple Auditorium where I performed in a skit called "Nepotism." This, according to local press reports, had been written by none other than Sherwood. Can you imagine? Now he was my manager *and* my writer. In truth, I'd written it myself, yet the really newsworthy aspect to that comedy sketch was that it costarred our kids Peter, Suzy, Stephanie, and Perry, as well as our longtime housekeeper, Mabel.

This sweet, vivacious little woman had been a part of our family for well over a decade, even following us from the West Coast to St. Louis after she had married and changed her surname from Bridgewater to Bess. However, since our arrival, there had been a hubbub among many of the WASP residents of Webster Groves because she was black—those bastards were something else. So, I could hardly blame Mabel when, in 1964, she decided to quit our household and move away. And I also can't say I was anything but delighted when her Norwegian replacement quickly attracted the beady eye of my celebrity husband.

Twenty-fifth wedding anniversary congratulations to Phyllis and Sherwood Diller. And he's a man of imagination. He bought Phyllis a solid gold cookie cutter in the shape of a star . . .
—Los Angeles Herald-Examiner, *November 10, 1964*

By now our whole marriage was a sham. While Sherry was screwing "Miss Norway," he was also bolstering his image as an international big shot by opening an account with the Hongkong and Shanghai Bank of California in the name of *Fang Diller*.

Can you believe it? I'd stumble upon the used checkbook many years later, but back then I had no idea because I was otherwise distracted—assiduously making plans to spend my life with Warde. Being Catholic, he wouldn't divorce his wife. She was, however, terminally ill, and in the early summer of 1965 she passed away. That July, I filed for divorce. I was appearing in the Empire Room at the Palmer House Hotel in Chicago when the press carried reports of the split, along with my explanation that this was due to "just plain old incompatibility." Talk about an understatement. At last I was free . . . or so I thought.

In my act, I had always referred to my fictional mother-in-law and fictional sister-in-law as Moby Dick and Captain Bligh. Well, *immediately* after I divorced Sherwood, Maude and Dr. Jeane sued me for a quarter-million dollars! They made me file a deposition, and even then their shyster lawyer—who was, of course, working on spec—told them, "You don't have a case." They were trying to say that I had specifically named *them* Moby Dick and Captain Bligh, and although I insisted these weren't real characters, the Dillers clearly wanted them to be. So, they did a pretty nasty thing. They had this lawyer inform every radio and television station in the country that I couldn't use that material. You see, they were really trying to hurt me. I would go around the country and find this out, and I'd say, "Look, relax. It's okay." And I just kept doing the material—what the hell.

Moby Dick was born on the eighth, ninth, and tenth of June.
When she was a kid, her mother used to dress her alike. She was
so big, she could only play seek. Now she lies around the house

and hums recipes. When she wears a white dress, we show
movies on her. The great big fat old bat—she went to the doctor
with a pain under her left breast. It turned out to be a trick
knee. . . . Captain Bligh is so skinny, she has to walk with her
knees together to keep her nylons up. When she wears a black
wig she looks like a ballpoint pen. The bags under her eyes are
her cheeks.

I'll never forget the deposition in St. Louis. I was there for an
hour with my New York lawyer, but when it came time for Maude
and Jeane's deposition they didn't show. They didn't want it.
They could never have gone through with it. So, we settled out
of court for $6,000 and I never stopped using those names, al-
though once they were no longer fresh, I just said "Fang's mother
and sister."

In the summer of 1965, making a clean break from my previous life, I finally decided to base myself in Los Angeles and move
the kids out there with me. Sherwood kept the house in Webster
Groves and an eight-unit apartment building in St. Louis that I
had purchased as an investment, along with a brand-new Thun-
derbird. I left him set up for life . . . You can pretty much guess
where this is heading.

Sherry would move into the apartment and, after living with
the Norwegian housekeeper for several years, he'd be dumped by
her. Next he'd marry one of his tenants, and the two of them
would come to see me play piano with the St. Louis Symphony.
They would also attend the Los Angeles wedding of our youngest
child, Perry, but after that I'd never see them again. Of course, it

wouldn't be long before Sherry would lose everything he owned. No matter what you gave him, it would be gone. He and wife number-two would move to L.A., and he'd eventually wake up one morning to discover that she had taken her car, half of the money out of the bank, and left him. Thereafter, he would periodically get in touch with one of our children living in the Valley, but basically he'd keep a low profile, and at the time of his death, he would have just $800—a sad but, I have to say, inevitable ending.

The last time Fang had a gleam in his eye, there was a short in his electric blanket. . . . I asked him to lower the thermostat. He put it six inches above the floor.

Before our separation, Red Skelton had put me on a $10,000 hold to ensure no one but his own production company could approach me about doing a sitcom. This was going to be about Phyllis and Fang, and everything was ready to go, but the minute I divorced Sherwood, I was told to keep the $10,000 and the project was shelved. Again, Sherry had been mistaken for Fang, and that was a shame because it might have been a hot show. Then again, since everyone had their own image of Fang, providing him with an on-screen face and voice may have also ruined my stage act. So, perhaps the magic was working in my favor.

In August 1965, I bought a twenty-two-room, English-style house on South Rockingham Avenue in the Brentwood section of L.A., and moved in there with Suzy, Stephanie, and Perry, as well as Warde and his two sons, Todd and Shane. Warde came from a fine family, which in itself was an added attraction. I was just crazy about his mother, a little round giggler and boozer named Teresa—she and I would laugh with tears in our eyes. She was so easy to make laugh and she was so mod, driving around in a sporty little sedan. I just adored her. Then there were Warde's brothers, both of whom had gone to Oxford and studied law. One was a Rhodes scholar and the other, Donn Tatum, would help to run Disney after Walt died, alongside Card Walker and Walt's brother, Roy. I wasn't used to having such incredible in-laws.

It was the Tatums who alerted me to the fact that the Rockingham house was for sale and who engineered my getting it. They said, "Boy, this is a deal, you'd better grab it," and I did. Built around a courtyard on an acre of secluded land, measuring just under 10,000 square feet, and providing me with an over-sized kitchen, numerous character-filled rooms, and ample space to store all of my costumes, this fabulous property, once owned by Republican Senator Lawrence C. Phipps, was the home I had dreamed of, the home I had written about so many years before, the icing on the cake. It was, I kept telling myself, what I deserved.

Just under a decade earlier, L.A. had felt like strange and hostile territory. Now, secure in my own position, I adapted easily to the laid-back, sun-drenched lifestyle alongside neighbors that included Robert Mitchum, Bette Davis, and Pat O'Brien. Judy Garland lived just a couple of doors away, and I remember one time when she was rushed to nearby St. John's Hospital to have her stomach pumped. The ambulance had windows and I could see Judy inside, flailing her arms and being restrained. Then, about four days later, another neighbor, Cloris Leachman, knocked on my door with a baby on her hip and told me that Judy was asking around for pills. I mean, Judy had only just dried out. And now here she was, desperate for more of the same. No doubt about it, this was a very different scene from Webster Groves. However, I *loved* my new home. And what's more, I was living here with my kids as well as with the man I adored.

Once again, I had no idea what I was letting myself in for.

Eight

GLITZ AND HOPE

My mid-sixties image makeover happened by accident. The wild hair, the loud dresses, the rhinestone-studded ankle boots—these helped grab the eye, ridicule my supposedly lousy figure, and convey an increasingly outrageous persona. Yet what turned out to be a sharp career move had simply evolved from a ham-fisted attempt to avert the one thing that's guaranteed to look worse than a guy losing his hair: a bald chick.

Warde always took such good care of his own appearance, every hair was perfectly in place. When he'd lie on the floor, he would put a Kleenex there and I'd ask, "Is that to protect the rug or your hair?" Since he was thinning on top he would visit a clinic in New York that supposedly helped prevent hair loss. My hair was even thinner. Having bleached it myself for the past seven years, I'd scorched and stripped it in a barbarian way. I never had the time to visit a beauty parlor, and in the beginning I'd never had enough money, but now I decided to visit that same place in New York where the experts might preserve what fried blond locks I had left. Their prescription? Lean over with my head down and, using a special hand-held rubber massage brush, briskly rub the scalp whenever I had a spare moment. This should stimulate regrowth.

Reasoning that I didn't have a whole lot to lose, either logically or folically, I massaged my scalp constantly in between making about ten daily radio and TV appearances in New York. The regrowth never happened. Yet, thanks to the special brush, my remaining hair stuck straight up in the air and before long my new "style" had caught on with audiences everywhere. It became a part of me, and it quickly grew increasingly outlandish until I adopted the fright wigs. More than ever, women who saw me perform could now feel beautiful by comparison, while their guys must have suddenly felt like they were living with Aphrodite.

I was in a beauty parlor and said to the guy, "I'm looking for a hairstyle that will simply drive men wild!" He said, "So am I."

So many great things have resulted from mistakes: my freakish hairdo, for one; me, for another. I sure as hell wasn't a planned child, I was a mistake, but look what a great life I've had. Once I'd stumbled upon a way to really indulge my longtime passion for clothes, I was able to have an absolute blast. After all, this was the Swinging Sixties, baby, so it was only natural for me to wear a whole bunch of colorful minidresses, and I also designed an array of glitzy ankle boots that became as much my trademark as the cigarette holder. The look may have been gaudy but it always contained elements of chic. I was *never* un-chic, although people didn't realize that. And I also felt that, with the bigger hair, I looked pretty good from certain angles. Just not from *every* angle.

I was never more aware of this than when watching myself on TV. *Oh, brother.* Still, it was television that continued to give me widespread exposure, and in 1963 I starred in my own ninety-minute *Phyllis Diller Special,* taped in New York during early November and aired by ABC on Thanksgiving night, just five days after President Kennedy's assassination. The nation was in no mood to laugh even if it desperately needed to, yet if the execs had their way the show wouldn't have aired at all.

We rehearsed for a week, everything was ready to go, but then the day before the shoot some ABC big shots came to the Waldorf and told me they wanted to scrap the whole thing. Less than impressed by what they had seen during rehearsals, they had got cold feet, but I stood my ground. "This is unacceptable," I stormed. "I'm going to call my astrologer!"

For a while I was into that kind of thing, although always with tongue in cheek, never believing it was cut-and-dried. In this case I thought it could serve as a means to an end, so I called my astrologer and asked, "Is tomorrow a good day for me to do the show? They want to cancel it." She said, "Well, there's confusion in the morning, but it's a great day." I then relayed this information to the execs, saying, "You know there's always confusion during the rehearsal, but it's going to be great," and the result was that the show went ahead and turned out to be quite a success. Oh darling, you have to admire my ingenuity.

While Warde crooned a couple of quiet numbers, the other guests included my son Peter playing banjo, Japanese singer Izumi Yukimura, and the comic ballroom dance team of Tanya and Biagi. Okay, so they weren't exactly big names outside their own household, but I wrote the entire show and, according to the *Chicago Tribune*, this proved I was "an adult comic with a fine sense of what is honestly funny about the world today."

The director had won a Peabody Award, so he was hot, but at one point, after Warde had really started to bug him, he came to me and said, "Get this guy off my back. Either he stops trying to direct or I'm outta here." Warde and I weren't even living together, yet he was already throwing his weight around. This should have served as a warning. I ignored it. During the shoot he missed a cue, which was terribly dangerous because we were filming live, and so I had to cover while somebody got him onstage. I'd soon learn this was typical. Both of my men had their idiosyncratic problems, and I always had to cover for them.

Fang, the idiot, was watching television one night and a guy was showing how to use a condom by putting on a sock. Now Fang is carrying a sock in his wallet.

The year before, during the run of *Wonderful Town*, there was an occasion when, seven minutes into the show, the leading man was supposed to make his first appearance, yet Warde was still at home writing letters. He had forgotten there was a Wednesday matinée! The production had to be closed down until he arrived by car, changed into his costume, and walked onstage, although by then a lot of the audience had left. What a mess. As I've mentioned, Warde's dumbness may have been due to brain damage caused by that fall out of a second-story window when he was two years old. He'd never graduated high school, even though his publicity bio stated that he had attended Oxford. What it failed to mention was that he'd simply gone there to visit his brothers.

Still, after breaking new ground with the *Phyllis Diller Special*, I also enjoyed a new high in April 1964 when I performed at the White House for Lady Bird Johnson. A woman who had served five presidents was retiring, and she'd been given a gold cigarette box with all of their signatures. Well, she was my biggest fan, and I just happened to be appearing at the Shoreham Hotel in Washington, so as a surprise for her they got me to visit 1600 Pennsylvania Avenue and put on a private show. Aside from Jack Kennedy, I'd get to meet all of the U.S. presidents from Eisenhower on. It's just a shame I wasn't around for FDR. With that cape and that cigarette holder he was my kinda guy!

By September 1964 I was fronting a weekly variety program on ABC, *Show Street*, which aired in the 10:30 to 11:00 Saturday nighttime slot that followed *The Hollywood Palace*. Whereas the *Palace*'s first outing of the season was hosted by Debbie Reynolds and featured stars like Liberace, Buddy Hackett, Rich Little, Stan Getz, Astrud Gilberto, and nine U.S. Olympic gymnasts, my showcase series for young talent kicked off with a satirical trio named Jim, Jake and Joan, and singers Sandy Contella and Lainie Kazan—Lainie was then a stand-in for Barbra Streisand in *Funny Girl* on Broadway.

> Show Street . . . *has managed to hang in nicely against net-work competition from* Gunsmoke *and NBC's Saturday night flicks . . . Comic Diller will be ankling the show anon, primarily because her far-flung nitery bookings necessitate a flight in every Sunday (to tape two segs at a crack), and this wear-and-tear is being felt. This GAC headliner hasn't been getting her top fee for fronting* Show Street*—it's understood to be a four-figure stipend; but as one insider cracks, "She's been getting damn good exposure for herself in the bargain."*
>
> —Variety, *December 9, 1964*

Was I ever. *Show Street* was a perfect vehicle for me, as well as for up-and-comers such as actor Robert Guillaume (when his surname was still Williams) and Spanish singer-dancer Charo. Tightly scripted and shot in a theater—which is the perfect setting for me, far better than a studio—it also provided Joan Rivers with her first TV-related job, working in the production office as a joke writer. However, it all came to an end when I asked for double pay. Perhaps I should have been a little less demanding, but I was stretched to the limit and had only my one day off from club engagements to rehearse and shoot a couple of shows, so it was awfully difficult.

By then, setting box-office records wherever I played—including Harrah's in Lake Tahoe and the Crescendo on the Sunset Strip—I was earning up to $15,000 a week. In America, there were two great rooms for comedy during the course of my career. One was at the Sands in Las Vegas, where the thrust stage was almost like being in the round—the Rat Pack could have never happened on a less intimate proscenium—and the other was the Sammy Davis Room at Harrah's in Reno. This is the most perfect room; the right shape, the right color, the right crew, and the right stage, with an indicator embedded in the floor to tell performers how long they've been on and how long there is to go. When you're doing comedy the laughs can make a difference to the show's structure, so this takes all the guesswork out of where you are.

Year after year, I'd buy comic lines for $5 a time and insert them in my routine. If they worked, they worked, and if they didn't, I'd keep walking. No one was *ever* able to write me a routine, aside from Gene Perret who wrote a small routine about a dog and worked for everyone out here, including Bob Hope, Bill Cosby, and Carol Burnett. Gene was one of my top writers.

I am the proud owner of the dumbest dog in the world. When I tell him to sit I have to show him which end to use. . . . If he sees a female in heat, he waits to be introduced. . . . It's embarrassing to have a German shepherd that bites its nails. . . . He leaks more than my 1959 Edsel. He should get good mileage from his legs because every time I see him, he's only using three of them.

I have been the first sale for so many comedy writers; people such as Pat McCormick who would later work for the *Tonight Show,* and Charlie Hauck who'd write for *Frasier.* I know how wonderful that first job is. And I've also received thousands of letters from the general public offering me gags. At one point I hired a couple of guys in Canada to go through all my mail and mark the ones that were old jokes, because I was spending *thousands* on old jokes. You see, when I first got in the business, I didn't know any old jokes.

The reason I'm not an alcoholic is I don't like to drink in front of the kids . . . and when you're away from them, who needs it?

That line was supplied to me by a Wisconsin housewife named Mary McBride, my other top writer, who would ghostwrite three of my four best-selling comedy books for Doubleday: *Phyllis Diller's Housekeeping Hints, Phyllis Diller's Marriage Manual,* and *The Complete Mother.* Mary lived in Janesville—she still does—and she had my laboratory right there. Again, after she sent me a joke in the mail I became her first employer, and she'd eventually carve out her own career as an author and guest speaker. This was more than fortunate since she was left to take care of five kids when her husband fell off a bicycle, hit his head, and died.

I had thousands of joke writers, both male and female, in the States, Canada, and Australia. Without realizing it I was running a thriving business, almost like a cottage industry, and Ingrid, my home assistant for more than twenty years, initially began working for me fresh out of UCLA just to update me on the contributions of people such as Mary Agnes Liddell of Los Altos, California, Larry DiGirolamo of Brackenridge, Pennsylvania, Robert Orben of Baldwin Harbor, New York, and Ray Rieves and Nonnee Coan of Norfolk, Virginia.

Still, I wrote at least seventy-five percent of all the material myself, and people often told me they loved to hear me say what they would have *loved* to say about the woman next door, the husband, the mother-in-law, whoever. In fact, my acerbic one-liners also reflected what *I* might think about people but never dared say to their faces, because I didn't want to hurt them and I didn't want to fight. My favorite joke has always been the triple whammy, where one line builds on another, each revealing something new about the idiots around me even though I'm clearly just as stupid. This isn't easy to create.

I realized on our first wedding anniversary that our marriage was in trouble. Fang gave me luggage. It was packed. My mother damn near suffocated!

Those last three sentences each take you in a different direction, and they're capped by a nice hard word; "suffocated!" It's all about alliteration and ending abruptly with a hard consonant— flick, Fang, cook—to emphasize the mock hostility. When complaining about the mother-in-law, I'd often mumble, "that old *bitch!*" Audiences loved it, and they also ate up a rapid-fire succession of one-liners on the same subject. I'd deliver one setup and then tag-tag-tag-tag-tag. That's economy. And my laugh would serve both as the cue and as the exclamation point.

My material was geared towards everyone of all ages and from different backgrounds, and I wanted to hit them right in the middle. I didn't want giggles—I could get those with my looks—I wanted boffs, and I wanted people to get the joke at the same moment and laugh together. That way I could leave everything to my timing. I didn't need to wait for a giggle here or a little titter there. One joke followed the other with a flow and a rhythm. It was like music, and I'd leave the audience to take charge of the laughs while, by picking things up at just the right moment, I'd ensure these never drowned out my next joke. Everything had a natural feel to it. I never rehearsed and I never, *ever* practiced in front of a mirror—the reflection alone would be enough to finish me. Talk about looking straight at the enemy.

I was doing mad business wherever I played. One time, I was working at the Chi Chi Club in Palm Springs and the place was jammed. Bob Hope called up and said he wanted to see me, and as there weren't any seats some people were thrown out of a booth to accommodate him. (They were probably given free drinks.) Another night, when he called the outdoor theater in Palm Springs to ask what time the movie started, the guy said, "Well, Mr. Hope, what time would you *like* it to start?" That's the kind of clout he enjoyed. It had been several years since our only other meeting, when I'd bombed at that horrible Lotus Club in Washington, D.C., so it was some kind of relief that he now saw me going over real big at the Chi Chi. It wouldn't be long before I'd meet him again.

A short time later, Bob and I flew together on a little shuttle plane from L.A. to Palm Springs. He sat beside me and during that half-hour trip we really got acquainted, talking about fans and autographs. When we arrived his housekeeper, Eileen Taylor, was there to collect him in a station wagon, and he had her take me home. Bob loved that housekeeper, and my characters in his movies were modeled after her. She was a skinny blond, not a pretty woman, and she was feisty and acerbic—someone really famous would be sitting at the end of the dining table, and she'd walk behind the guy and roll her eyes to express her disapproval. It didn't matter who it was, she'd just roll them as if to say, "*Oh, Jesus.*" After all, some of those people could be full of shit, yet nothing fazed her and nothing really got past her. She had her own ideas and she let them be known. Well, in the three movies in which I appeared with Bob, I portrayed someone serving him—a maid, a babysitter, and a nurse—and I know that I was patterned after Eileen.

Would you believe that I once entered a beauty contest? I must have been out of my mind. I not only came in last, I got 361 get-well cards.

The first few times he and I worked together was on his TV specials, and pretty soon we became fast friends. There was immediate chemistry between us. In fact, the equivalent of sex with

Warde was intellect with Hope. We could talk on any level, and it was reciprocal and strong. When you meet a person who is in complete simpatico with all your views and there is mutual admiration—and boy, did we have *that*—then it's magic. I mean, hey baby, everyone admired him, but for him to admire me was something else. He was just about the only person I've ever known for whom the word *icon* was an apt description.

Bob taught me a lot about comedy, explaining cause and effect as well as the motivations behind a comic persona—thanks to him, I learned where to pause and break on a line that I'd normally say all in one breath, turning an ordinary quip into something memorable. Previously, I had copied him without even realizing it, because I tried to avoid copying *anyone*. And what's more, he liked to make jibes about people and I liked to be on the receiving end, so we were terrific foils, complementing each other perfectly. Not for nothing had newspaper columnists been labeling me "the female Bob Hope."

Off-camera, offstage he was a very natural guy, not one of those fools who's "on" all the time. For him acting funny was a profession, but he was also warm, witty, and full of fun in real life. The one-liners just poured out of him, and he had a funny attitude. He was also a most positive person, although we had such a close relationship that on a couple of occasions I was treated to his behind-the-scenes lines. Those were rare for him. I remember a woman singing badly at a nightclub and him saying something derogatory out of the side of his mouth. That kind of thing only slipped out because he could trust me, and he knew I was thinking the same.

Throughout the years, while we appeared together in three movies and twenty-two TV specials, Bob was mad about me and I was nuts about him; yet nothing ever happened between us. I knew a relationship was an impossibility. Then again, I also have a theory that I reminded him of his mother. She sang and played the piano, and when I saw a picture of her I thought we resembled one another. That's why he always preferred my old face, pre-plastic surgery. (I should have given it to him for Christmas, but the dog ate it and was terribly ill. That was the first time I ever saw a dog spit up a fur ball.)

Bob just wanted me around all the time, whether it was at a golf tournament or in a show, and he'd always send private jets to fly me in. He once gave me a great big picture of a toad bearing the inscription KISS A TOAD TONIGHT, and at the bottom he signed it: Toad Hope. His wife, Dolores, and her mother, Teresa, were very much aware of how he felt. One time, when we were going to the racetrack, Bob was in the front seat alongside the driver, I was in the back with Dolores and Teresa, and the old girl said something to the effect of "Keep away from him. Don't get any ideas." Always count on an old lady to speak her mind. Still, the whole family accepted me and I was almost one of them.

In September 1965, Bob and I began shooting *Boy, Did I Get a Wrong Number!* and I was so thrilled. I considered it my first real movie, even though a few months earlier I'd starred in *The Fat Spy* alongside Jayne Mansfield and Jack E. Leonard, that acerbic nightclub comic who predated Don Rickles as King of the Insult. A supposed spoof of the teenage "beach party" films that were then all the rage, it had to be one of the *worst* things ever committed to celluloid, full of lousy jokes and terrible music. Suffice it to say that, as Camille Salamander, I was one of several characters heading for a desert island rumored to contain the fountain of youth—what a bust. And that's about all I could say for Jayne Mansfield, too. The fifties sex bomb with the blond hair and 40-D boobs was by then overweight, hooked on pills, and firmly on the skids. All of her lines were on cue cards. But then, so were everyone else's.

The filming, such as it was, took place in Cape Coral, Florida, and I felt as if I was in the hellhole of America—if they ever give this country an enema, they should stick it in Cape Coral. There was so much humidity that everyone was bathed in sweat, and, thanks to all the mosquitoes, poor old Jack E. Leonard had to take several days off after being bitten on the lips and on his bald head. Every day at four o'clock we'd stop shooting while a crop duster flew overhead and sprayed a chemical to kill those pests. Still, I was receiving a tidy sum to star in this turkey, so I was tickled pink. That was, until I saw the finished movie while fulfilling an engagement in Las Vegas—I crawled out of the theater. *Crawled*.

Boy, Did I Get a Wrong Number! was, thankfully, an altogether different experience, even though, having worked on *The Fat Spy* as well as a few TV shows with Hope, I assumed there would be cue cards. There weren't. He and everybody else learned their lines . . . except me. Look how dumb I was. I arrived on the set and, since I was about to appear in the first scene, there was no precedent for me to know there wouldn't be cue cards. Can you imagine the feeling of panic? Oh baby, I learned my lines so fast. They didn't shut down the set because I never let on that I was in trouble. I just got hold of a script and . . . talk about a fast study. I crammed everything right then and there and we got through that first scene; one where I was washing dishes, looking at them in a Dillerish way, and wiping them on my butt.

In another scene, shot on location at Big Bear Lake in the San Bernardino National Forest, I was supposed to ride a motorcycle and naturally I had a double. Well, the girl who was doubling for me unfortunately broke her leg while attempting a particularly difficult maneuver and she was replaced by a very petite guy. He was standing around one day when we broke for lunch, and Warde, who had just arrived to visit me on the set, saw my looka-like, grabbed him from behind, spun him around, and kissed him on the lips. Since the guy was wearing a fright wig and the same clothes as me, what did he expect?

The movie itself was, I thought, just darling, and it still plays constantly in this country. A bedroom farce in which Hope gets entangled with a movie starlet portrayed by Elke Sommer, it features me as an acerbic, incompetent maid named Lily—like Eileen Taylor, I am very much part of the family, always letting everyone know what *I* think. Elke, meanwhile, is so roundly cute, she does a marvelous job portraying herself, and Marjorie Lord is fabulous as Hope's delicate wife. In *Eight on the Lam*, again directed by George Marshall, I'd portray a babysitter named Golda opposite Hope and Jonathan Winters, while in *The Private Navy of Sgt. O'Farrell*, I'd pursue Bob as sex-starved nurse Nellie Krause. I don't know if you could say I was cast according to type, but it worked for *me*.

When *Boy, Did I Get a Wrong Number!* was released in the summer of 1966 I was at my peak, and six months later I joined Bob on his Christmas USO Tour of Vietnam, Thailand, and Guam, along with bandleader Les Brown, singers Anita Bryant and Vic Damone, singer/dancer/actress Joey Heatherton, bathing-suited baton twirler Diana Shelton, dance trio The Korean Kittens, and reigning Miss World, Reita Faria. This was a huge, magnificent endeavor, and Bob had it completely under control thanks to all the backing that anyone could ever want: the U.S. Government, NBC, his hand-picked performers, and a bunch of terrific writers.

The tour entailed a long, long trip undertaken in a huge transport that felt like we were flying in a basement. There were no windows, wires and pipes were steaming and dripping, and everything was fashioned out of gray metal. That thing wasn't intended to attract tourists. Still, we spent a week based out of Bangkok, one night sleeping on an aircraft carrier before doing a show, and for several days we also visited hospitals where the sight that greeted us was just heartbreaking. I found it really difficult to be cheerful around people who had been horribly wounded, and at one point Hope took me aside and said, "Now look, you can't break down and allow them to see you so sad." I hadn't cried in front of them but I also hadn't been too cheerful, and as Bob explained, you shouldn't sympathize, you should try to joke and lift their spirits.

29 Dec, 1966

Miss Diller:

Please accept these flowers as a token of my appreciation for coming over to Clark. I was stationed at Scott AFB, Illinois, outside St. Louis for five years, and always wanted the chance to see you in person. I enjoy you very much, you remind me of my mother! Thank you, Miss Diller.

A great fan of yours,

A/C Donald S. Shirk

USAF Hospital

Clark Air Force Base, Philippines

At every show, the front row would have people in beds on IV's. We had a serious job to do, yet my first effort at entertaining turned out to be all wrong. My material was for the home people, it was not for the people out there fighting a war, and I was the first person to realize this. However, here is an example of Hope's generosity: he had the writers come up with a whole new routine where he worked as my straight man while I got all the jokes. It was as if we were a snippy married couple, along the lines of the Bickersons, and that kept me in the show, although I did also appear in other scenes, of course.

At night, after the shows, we'd attend these wonderful parties where the top person in a particular area would host and entertain our troops at dinner. There was the Queen of Thailand and also the young King of Siam who played the saxophone and who joined in with the Les Brown Band. What a night *that* was, filled with talk, laughter, music, and exotic food. These were the little thank-you's for being there. On Christmas Day, we performed in Saigon, and I can remember having dinner that night in a hotel and looking out the window to see flares in the sky. There was, after all, a war going on. We used to ride in these huge helicopter transports that could seat around forty passengers, and beside each window towards the front was a gunner. Still, it was a magnificent tour.

One should never tap a Vietnamese on the head. Undoubtedly, it will be taken as a personal injury to the individual's human dignity and possibly as a blow to his ancestors as well. Reserve any friendly pats on the back for intimate friends who have long been exposed to foreigners. Better still, keep hands off if you don't want to offend a Vietnamese. . . . Whatever you do, be careful on how you use your hand in motioning someone toward you. You're sure to get a dirty look or worse if you hold your palm up and wriggle your fingers in signalling to someone. The sign is ordinarily used in Vietnam to attract the attention of dogs and children.

—*Excerpt from a list of "Vietnamese Customs,"*
supplied by the U.S. Army

Several months earlier, riding the crest of a professional wave, I had been approached by ABC about starring in my own sitcom. Running last in a three-way race with CBS and NBC, the network was searching for a female comic who might attract viewers in the same way that Lucille Ball had done for CBS. Accordingly, Filmways Productions, the company responsible for *Mr. Ed*, *The Beverly Hillbillies*, and *The Addams Family*, was commissioned to develop a vehicle for me, and the result was *The Pruitts of Southampton*.

Adapted from the novel *House Party* by Patrick Dennis, this show was based on a cute if implausible idea: after a widowed Long Island socialite named Phyllis Pruitt discovers she owes $10 million in back taxes, she and her family are conveniently allowed to continue living inside their sixty-room Southampton mansion. The Internal Revenue Service, you see, fears that knowledge of the Pruitts' financial plight might cause a stock-market crash—hey, no one said this was reality TV—so Phyllis takes it upon herself to concoct ideas, many of them harebrained, that will preserve the wealthy image and keep her family afloat.

The Pruitts of Southampton was, in essence, the complete opposite of *The Beverly Hillbillies*. (I never realized it back then, but it also partly echoed the situation that my former Diller in-laws had found themselves in many years before, trying to keep up appearances despite going broke.) Filmed in Hollywood while exteriors of the mansion were shot at the famed Biltmore House in Asheville, North Carolina, the show went into production at around the same time as *The Addams Family* was winding down, and Warde was insanely jealous because *he* wasn't in the cast. This included veteran character actors Reginald Gardiner as old Uncle Ned and Grady Sutton as Sturgis the butler; Pam Freeman as my twenty-two-year-old daughter, Stephanie; and none other than Gypsy Rose Lee as my nauseatingly nosy neighbor Regina Wentworth.

I got to know Gypsy really well while filming the series, and we became very close friends. She kept bringing me gifts that she had made by hand—remember, her mother had made all of the family's clothes and costumes, including her stripper gloves and coats made out of blankets stolen from hotels. Among the things that I still cherish are a scarf and matching gloves that were handmade for me by Gypsy. Nevertheless, she was a character and she could be difficult. One day in makeup, she screamed with pain and the hair guy said, "I haven't even touched you," to which she replied, "But you're going to."

Another time, she had her own show on KGO-TV in San Francisco, directed by a young Marty Pasetta who would subsequently become a Hollywood institution. Well, one day I made a guest appearance and he actually quit on air. He stormed out of the booth and told Gypsy to go to hell. He'd had it with her. And although what he did was very unprofessional, it was certainly dramatic—the viewers could hear the entire thing. Marty left town, went to L.A., and never looked back, directing everything from Elvis Presley and Frank Sinatra TV specials to live broadcasts of the Grammys and Academy Awards.

Without a doubt Gypsy wasn't easy, yet on *The Pruitts of Southampton* she pretty much kowtowed to me. She was just happy to be booked. The series began airing in September 1966, yet it did nothing in the ratings opposite CBS's *The Red Skelton Show* and NBC's theatrical movies, and the following January it switched from its Tuesday night time slot to a Friday night one, the title was changed to *The Phyllis Diller Show*, the mansion was replaced by an upscale boardinghouse that was intended to help pay off the government, and several new people were added to the cast: John Astin as my son, Rudy (which would have entailed me being a twelve-year-old mother); Paul Lynde as my good-for-nothing brother, Harvey; Marty Ingels as handyman boarder Norman Krump; and Richard Deacon as the tax man, Mr. Baldwin. Still, by the end of September 1967 the show was off the air, and this wasn't just due to poor ratings. I had walked.

Filming everything like a movie made the whole enterprise a lot more difficult. The crew had to move walls, set up intricate lighting, and shoot everything three times; a master shot that ran from the beginning to end of each scene, and then the close-ups. It was a very laborious way to work, entailing seventeen-hour days and nightly homework learning seventeen pages of script, none of which was helped by the fact that I hated the script girl and she obviously hated me. She wouldn't let me change a comma. I wasn't involved in writing the script but it was *my* show, and she should never have had that kind of power. I should have had her fired the first day, but again, avoiding confrontation, I did nothing. That was a mistake.

Every now and then I would get a director with whom I was completely in tune, and that would be wonderful, but there was also one whom I just couldn't stand. I'm not a physical comic, yet he seemed intent on turning me into Carol Burnett, insisting that I embellish whatever I was saying with various bits of physical business. That didn't come naturally to me. Then there was a huge old Rolls-Royce limousine mounted on apple boxes, setting up a joke where I was supposed to go under the car and try to fix it, but with my feet sticking out and my boots facing down towards the floor. Well, I was placed underneath the car and I re-alized it was touching me, so I had the crew bring me back out and I told the director, "I can't do this scene. The car is way too close for comfort." He said, "What do you drink, Phyllis? Here, have a vodka." His idea was to get me drunk enough to do the scene, but I refused and went back to my bungalow, and while I was in there the car collapsed. I would have been dead at the age of forty-nine, crushed beneath the body of that big old Rolls Phantom.

I am in my fourteenth year of a ten-day beauty plan. When I go to bed at night, I've got so much grease on my body, I wear snow chains to hold up my gown . . . I hope skirts don't get any shorter—my legs don't go all the way up.

The most permanent director was Neil Simon's brother, Danny, and he always appeared to be so unsure, as if he hadn't prepared in advance. He'd be thinking about things on the set, and to me this wasn't proper helmsmanship. Still, the day I quit was when they handed me half a script. That really pissed me off. I couldn't reconcile myself to a modus operandi where they were writing while we were shooting, so I decided enough was enough. From the outset, I should have been more involved with the produc-tion side of things, but did I learn? Obviously not, because I quickly made the same mistake with my variety series, *The Beautiful Phyl-lis Diller Show.*

Broadcast by NBC on Sunday nights at ten, this ran for just fifteen weeks, from September through December 1968, and I

participated in everything, including the introductory monologue, the comedy sketches, and a whole assortment of musical
numbers. Comics Norm Crosby and Rip Taylor served as my regular support along with a young song-and-dance outfit named
the Curtain Calls, whom the producers hoped would turn into
the Osmonds, those toothy kids on *The Andy Williams Show*.
There was no way. The Osmonds were so talented.

Each week the Jack Elliott Orchestra and Jack Regas Dancers
performed a big production-number salute to such forgotten
icons as famed botanist Luther Burbank, fifteenth-century Spanish explorer Ponce de León, and nineteenth-century U.S. President Millard Fillmore. Researched by a staff that included my
son Peter, and written by the very talented Ed Scott, these musical set pieces were meant to be a joke, yet I'm not sure that anyone really got it. The viewers were probably too preoccupied
watching me try to dance. Well, I can't dance, and not even an
entire week spent putting me through my paces could change
that. I should have known better. What's more, I didn't like the
fact that one of the producers was *shtooping* one of the dancers—
big surprise that she had a speaking line every now and again!
Everything was wrong with that show.

My least favorite color is blue, my least favorite shape is
square—red and round are my whole thing. However, since no
one ever consulted me about the main stage backdrop, it was
adorned with hundreds of little blue flowers in squares. Then
there was the new bleacher system that didn't touch the floor. It
was supposed to be moved mechanically so that the crew could
reconfigure the audience seating according to our stage setup, yet

it never worked. Here were all these hefty guys struggling to push the thing around, and it was a disaster. And then there was the lighting man whom I should have had fired on the first day; a pint-sized queen who'd be up in the rigging, taking forever to get everything just right. Talk about a little power going a long way—Hitler with lights. I felt like saying, "Give me a gun."

During one of the shows, while I was performing in front of the audience, my secretary Corinne Carr actually had to restrain the guy who was in charge of our budget from walking onstage. For some reason that drunken bastard was after me, and he couldn't wait to say his piece. Never mind that, whenever we'd reach a crucial point in the taping, the union would call a break, even at *one in the morning*. Bob Finkel was my executive producer, yet he never did a thing to help. He was just a figurehead. And neither he nor the guys under him ever consulted me about the guests on my show, resulting in a lot of people whom I didn't want. One such person was the Danish-born comic pianist Victor Borge. Since my teens I had been such a great fan of his, but then I'd met him and he had been rude to me—sitting next to him in the piano bar at the old Garden of Allah in West Hollywood, I had asked, "Why are you in town?" to which he'd pointedly replied, "To hear the music." Nice.

Now, here we were several years later, Borge was a guest on my show, and he was supposed to do something new. However, he did the same routine that he had performed ever since settling in this country; the only routine he ever knew, playing a few bars of classical music and reading a piece of literature where he'd loudly blurt out sounds representing every comma and period. Well, screw him. Another time, the producers got a football player on the show, somebody whose name I'd never heard, and, boy, did they run into trouble with *him*. When the director said, "Walk over there, look that way," he growled, "I ain't goin' over there and you don't tell *me* where to look!" Immediately, I held his hand while pretending I adored quarterbacks, and he eventually went along with the whole routine. However, I would have never booked him. I was a comic, not a nursemaid or shrink.

Some of the other guests were fine—Ray Charles, Sonny & Cher—yet Zsa Zsa Gabor made a big scene when dye from the red feathers on her costume stained her arm. It was nothing, but you'd have thought she was taking her last breath, and, of course, she made sure this happened with the door to her dressing room wide open. *Pul-lease*. Kate Smith was also a problem. The over-sized singer of "When the Moon Comes Over the Mountain" and, most famously, "God Bless America," refused to wear the dress that had been designed for both her and me, insisted on taking time off to attend church, and was so nervous or paranoid that she locked herself in a room with her manager. Once again, trying to get things on track, I connected with her by telling a whole bunch of Polish jokes that—in the days before political correctness—were doing the rounds at the same time as the English were telling Irish jokes, the Canadians were telling Newfie jokes, and the French were telling Belgian jokes. In my case, they could just as easily have been Fang jokes, but at least they got Kate laughing and broke her down.

Did you hear about the Polish loan shark who lent out all his money and then skipped town? Or the Polish husband who, on discovering his wife in bed with his best friend, rushed to the closet, pulled out a gun, and pointed it at himself? When the wife started to giggle, he shouted, "Don't laugh! You're next!"

Throughout the sixties, as my career went into overdrive, you might think my lifestyle changed drastically in terms of the circles in which I was moving. Yet, I didn't have time to move in any circles. No time at all, although that's not to say I was without company. I'll never forget when I was playing Vegas—and had signed to do *The Beautiful Phyllis Diller Show* for NBC—all the people who aspired to get on the show came to Vegas, and I never picked up so many checks in my life. I also never received so many bouquets of red roses. It was ridiculous. Singer-actor Rudy Vallee had become a good friend, but he grew to hate me because he thought I was responsible for his not being on the show. It was the producers who weren't interested—he was completely out of date—but he didn't know this. The fact that I also didn't want him on the show was neither here nor there. His presence would have ruined things even more than they were already ruined. You don't book people because they're you're friends; but when you're on top, they think you should do whatever they ask.

The mother of my secretary, Corinne, was my double and my stand-in. All she had to do was stand in when they were setting up the lights, but with the cue cards all around she also couldn't resist speaking some lines. She was forever auditioning, forever hoping she was going to be discovered. Oh, the egos and the *non-sense*. I wasn't cut out for any of that. *The Beautiful Phyllis Diller Show* had some incredible writers, including Bob Weiskopf and Bob Schiller, whose other TV credits have included *I Love Lucy*, *All in the Family*, *The Flip Wilson Show*, *The Red Skelton Show*, *The Carol Burnett Show*, and *Maude*; my head guy, Gene Perret; and future *Saturday Night Live* producer Lorne Michaels. Yet, competing with ABC's Sunday movie showcase and the CBS action series *Mission Impossible*, it really didn't stand a chance.

I'm not the kind of person who enjoys power; not a Lucy or a Streisand who knows it all and does it all. I just hoped that things would go the way I wanted, yet that never happens unless you get real lucky. In that regard, I never got lucky. And I was also too distracted to find the will or the way to take a stand against many of the production decisions and try to turn things around.

There were, you see, major problems at home.

Nine

A DAME AND
A DRUNK

On this happy day
We are thankful
For our blessings
And we pray
For renewed belief
In ourselves
And each other
And hope
This bond of love
Will expand
To envelop
The entire universe

It was on a hot summer morning in Chicago, while Warde was attending Catholic Mass and I was in the middle of an engagement at the Palmer House in downtown's Loop, that I wrote "My Prayer." I needed it.

Once, at three a.m., I smelled smoke in our room and saw flames coming out of the heater. I woke Warde (who would have otherwise slept through it and died) and he called the front desk: "We have a fire in our room." The operator said, "Who *is* this?" Talk about a lousy attitude. Still, the fire department was contacted and soon we heard sirens—it's a terrible thing when you hear fire trucks approaching your hotel and know they're for you. All that the firemen were interested in was meeting me . . . at three in the morning—"Ooh, what a fun thing!" We had a magnificent suite with a living room, a kitchen, a dining room, and a bedroom, so I hid in the kitchen while those tall and handsome hunks put out the fire: *my* fire.

Another time, again at the Palmer House, I was with my dress designer, Omar, and after the show I gouged a deep hole in my left hand while using a knife to open a champagne bottle. Not a great idea. Thank God that Omar had worked as a nurse. I was bleeding rather badly, so she put a tourniquet on my upper arm and, because I'm always concerned about not dirtying anything, I sat on the floor and stuck my hand in the champagne's bucket of ice water. Omar then called someone to come and get me, but when two security guards sauntered in and saw my hand in a bucket of blood they assumed I had slit my wrist. After all, isn't that what we showbiz types always do?

The next thing I knew, these two idiots were rushing me to the hospital . . . or somewhere, because at first they couldn't find their way. It's fortunate that I was bleeding to death *slowly*. When I arrived at the emergency room, with my hand wrapped in a towel, everyone was obviously thinking, "Suicide!" On seeing the doctor, I told him "I don't want any stitches." Forget the skewered hand—I didn't want to be hurt. (I am *so* delicate.) In the end I was given five stitches and I was lucky. Had the knife gone a little further my future career as a concert pianist would have never happened. "My Prayer" paid dividends.

For me those few inspirational lines were about the importance of concentrating on what you have instead of what you don't have; a simple message addressed to the ether, to the cosmos, to me. To the power that is within all of us. To the Force. Subsequently set to music by Brentwood Symphony Orchestra founder Alvin Mills for a soprano voice, and then revised by me to be more personal—"On this happy day *I* am thankful for *my* blessings, and *I* pray for renewed belief in *myself* and *others* . . ."— it is my mantra; a mantra that has reflected and reinforced my positive outlook through the best and very worst of times.

My second marriage encompassed both.

Subconsciously, I knew from the beginning that Warde was bisexual. He didn't act effeminate but he had *the look*. It was in his eyes, in his smile, and—as the fashions became more colorful and flamboyant—in the way he dressed. Eventually, he transformed himself into something of a dandy. Since he didn't look that way when I met him, I may have been responsible, letting him do whatever he wanted—boy, did he love it when the Nehru look came in. Of course, he could wear anything, because he had the physique and the looks. What a *bod*. And I foolishly thought our marriage would straighten him out. A lot of women think like that, while others like being married to gay men. In fact, whenever music is mixed with gay, there's a good chance I'll be hooked, yet I *hated* it when that side of Warde became impossible to ignore. Forget the "bisexual" label. He was gay, but with the kind of family he was born into, it was a case of "You'd better get married and make this look good."

During our courtship we'd meet at different locations around the world and have such fun together. I didn't have a clue what he got up to when I wasn't around, and I was so madly in love with the guy that I didn't *want* to know. If I had been smart, I wouldn't have had a thing to do with him. Instead, I was as thick as bricks when it came to relationships, so we had an amazing time in the sack and that was that.

Once, when we were staying at the Waldorf Towers in New York, there was a guy with whom I suspected he was doing it; a pianist who had a nice little apartment in the city. However, when I confronted Warde about this, he picked up a chair in our suite and smashed it on the floor. Of course, I had to pay for that. He was the only person I ever confronted, and we had plenty of similar scenes, many of them thanks to a creep named Brother John.

A former CBS executive, John was a red-faced drunk who claimed to be a Catholic Brother in charge of boys. I *bet* he was. Oh, I *hated* Brother John. He was always in New York when we were there, and I had a fair idea he was screwing Warde. However, I wanted Warde so bad that I chose to overlook the possibility that he might be straying. That was, until our wedding day, October 7, 1965, when he wouldn't allow pictures to be taken. It was only thanks to my matron of honor, Wanda Ramey, that a few shots were snapped by her husband, yet they never ran anywhere because Warde didn't want them to. My gown had been in the making for almost a year, I'd shopped all over America for the right hat and shoes, and now there weren't going to be any pictures? His behavior was a real shock to me. My theory is that he didn't want any of his gay friends to know he'd got married, and he also didn't want anyone else to see him in the company of Brother John with whom he probably hoped to enjoy a *ménage à trois*.

Warde had Brother John use my Rolls-Royce to drive Stephanie and Suzanne from St. Louis to L.A., and pretty soon that apoplectic-looking sonofabitch began taking over—when he became involved in the refurbishment of my new home, I decided enough was enough. The guy was deciding which oven should be installed in the kitchen, for chrissakes! I wanted him out of there. Still, I remember getting home from the road one time and Suzy immediately taking me aside to describe how Warde and Brother John had locked themselves in our bedroom for over an hour. I said, "That's it!" I filed for divorce immediately. We had been married just three months.

At that time, it took one year for a divorce to become final, and during that year Brother John cared for Teresa, Warde's elderly mother whom I absolutely adored. She was living with the two of them in a Wilshire Corridor high-rise that I affectionately referred to as the Menopause Towers, and all three then moved to a little house that she purchased in Brentwood. I never saw Warde throughout that entire time. However, just one day before the divorce became final, I was heading along Sunset Boulevard and, out of the corner of my eye, I noticed Brother John sitting at a bus stop. I didn't acknowledge him but he obviously spotted me, because about seven o'clock that night I received a telegram from Warde: "May I come over and see you?" I called him immediately: "Okay." Does the word *stupid* spring to mind? As I keep saying, it's all about timing—there had been just one day to go and now I was jumping straight back into the fire. *Oh, God.*

My problem was the physical attraction. It was so strong, I couldn't resist. I didn't even bother getting Warde to apologize or promise to change his lifestyle—as my mother used to say, that would have been like stirring a turd. Why look back? Just move forward. What a joke. Brother John stopped hanging around, but little else changed, and I'd end up kicking Warde out a couple more times due to some pretty monstrous incidents.

Some bad things have been happening lately. A pervert called me. Five times. Collect. And that damn fool won't tell me where he lives.

The most upset I ever got was during one trip to Australia when I was scheduled to perform at a large hotel. My Australian audiences were the greatest—they were starved for comedy and they were laughers. It was like taking candy from a baby. Warde was my opening act and we went straight from the airport to the hotel following a long, exhausting flight from Los Angeles. Our limo driver was young, stocky, and good-looking, but I didn't give this much thought until I found myself being dropped off at the hotel while Warde went to a beach with the guy and blew him. I knew this because he returned with the smell of semen on his breath.

The famous Australian ballet dancer Sir Robert Helpmann was in the suite next door, and he must have heard every word as I sat the Great Lover down and proceeded to rant and rave for more than an hour. The air was blue with curse words: *my* curse words. There was no conversation because my drunk, contrite husband never said a thing. He just sat and listened while I blew my stack. *Blew my stack.* Normally, I never did that, but I was crazy about the man and I cared. With Sherwood it had been different. He had been so mean and such a do-nothing dummy that I never gave a damn. The Australian incident with Warde was the worst.

Here I was, living with a gorgeous guy who was gay, insecure, and a terrible alcoholic. From the first time I'd met him he had always been a drinker, but again I must have been in some sort of denial. I mean, on one trip to London we bought a heavy leather bag in which to carry his booze. It was a *booze bag*, and it went with him wherever he traveled. I also enjoyed drinking, but not as much as he and never in a manner that interfered with my work. I never, *ever* drank before a show.

To make matters worse, all was not well with the kids. Upset by my breakup with Sherry and my marriage to Warde, twenty-year-old Suzy and seventeen-year-old Stephanie had taken off and moved to San Francisco, where they lived together in an apartment. They really didn't approve of the setup on South Rockingham. And although we even had Sally here for a short time, monitored by a girl who was hired to take care of her, again it never worked out. Meanwhile, Warde's oldest child, Shane, yelled a lot, and I wouldn't stand for that. I still don't. I won't tolerate any raising of voices. That's why my home has thirteen phones—you can call between rooms, you don't have to shout. Eighteen-year-old Shane had been allowed to yell, so that was an issue, and I also never trusted him. To my mind he used people, but as usual I tried to gloss things over . . . until it just wasn't possible.

After Warde and Perry had a screaming argument in the driveway at the back of the house, Perry moved out. Twenty years old, he had dropped out of college at the end of his first year, and now that he had left home he would never return. I'd spent much of my adult life trying to get a nice place for my kids, and within a short time they were all gone. Warde, you see, considered himself the king of the roost—echoes of Sherwood. I sure knew how to pick them. If you repeat errors, you often repeat terrible errors. It would take me a lifetime to realize this.

Thank God that, throughout these years, I had plenty of incredible work to distract me. I was performing at clubs and concert venues all over the world, and in between there were tons of TV engagements, as well as an intriguing film: the 1969 big-screen adaption of Elmer Rice's brilliant 1923 expressionist satire *The Adding Machine*. Depicting technology's impact on American business, this focused on a department-store accountant named Mr. Zero who murders his boss after discovering he's being replaced by a computer. Zero is executed for his crime and, once in Heaven, he is then forced to contemplate his sorry existence. However, he learns nothing aside from the fact that he must return to Earth and do the whole thing over again.

The writer, producer, and director of this film was a protégé of Charlie Chaplin's named Jerome Epstein, who had coproduced Charlie's final movie projects: *A King in New York* and *A Countess from Hong Kong.* Jerome saw me onstage in London and asked me right then and there to costar as Zero's bored, moaning, unsympathetic wife. (I always land the glamor roles.) This resulted in six weeks at Shepperton Studios, a few miles southwest of London, working with a wonderful cast that included Billie Whitelaw, Charlie's son Sydney, and, as the main antihero, that terrific Irish actor, Milo O'Shea.

The film basically has two halves: mine and Zero's. Once he goes to Heaven, I'm never seen again. That's a mistake. Jerome never realized the film was overlong until its release, yet *The Adding Machine* represented a whole new area for me and I received good notices, even though the dramatic acting was difficult. I had no coaching; I just did it. My thing is comedy. Every fiber of my body is comedy. It is comedy that sustains me. So, I returned to that and never looked back.

Through Sydney Chaplin, I became friends with his sister Geraldine, and shortly afterwards I was invited to her wedding at the family home in Vevey, Switzerland. There were four hundred guests at dinner, most of whom had arrived in their own planes, including many of the crowned heads of Europe. I couldn't tell one from the other, but it was such a thrill to meet Charlie, a white-haired little man with an infectious smile. Sydney, on the other hand, could be a complete asshole. Thanks to him, I got thrown out of a London club owned by drag artist Danny LaRue. Sydney got so drunk, and had such a loud and foul mouth, that we were asked to leave. Between him and Warde, I was growing used to this behavior, but I sure as hell couldn't accept it.

In 1970, I signed to star for three months on Broadway as meddling matchmaker Dolly Gallagher Levi in *Hello, Dolly!* Oh honey, was that ever a high point. It had always been my great dream to play Broadway, and once again my dream came true. Performing at the Americana Hotel's Royal Box nightclub when it was *the* place to play, I had been invited to meet legendary producer David Merrick, the Tony Award–winning "Indomitable Showman," who duly announced that he wanted either me or Debbie Reynolds for the lead. *Me or Debbie Reynolds?* Talk about a contrast. I never realized he was joking until I repeated this to Bob Hope and he burst out laughing. You can tell how innocent I still was.

As it happens, Merrick had already approached Jack Benny to play Dolly in drag opposite George Burns as "unmarried half-a-millionaire" Horace Vandergelder. That would have been the greatest thing to ever happen on Broadway. Three years earlier, when interest in the show had been flagging, David had taken a major risk by recasting it with an all-black company led by Pearl Bailey and Cab Calloway. His gamble had paid off, and now he wanted to turn things on their head yet again with Benny and

Burns. It's a real shame this fantastic idea never materialized, but it turned into gold for me when my name was suggested by composer, stage director, and playwright Abe Burrows, the father of *Cheers* co-creator James Burrows. I wasn't even aware that Abe knew me, but Merrick took his advice—he clearly wasn't looking for a cutie like Betty Grable, who had previously succeeded Carol Channing, Ginger Rogers, and Martha Raye as Dolly.

Imagine me playing Dolly. That's like Joe Namath playing quarterback for the Jesuits. The only reason I was hired is because they wanted to get me on Broadway before everything went nude. I would never take off my clothes on stage. Why make the critics' job easy?

I was so thrilled to be invited, I took a cut in salary. I wanted Jerry Herman's musical on my résumé. Richard Deacon—who had portrayed the tax man in my sitcom *The Pruitts of Southampton*—was cast, thanks to me, but I'd end up being sorry. I should have left it to those people who knew Broadway to choose a Vandergelder. Instead, I suggested Richard, they accepted, and during one of the very first rehearsals he got into it with the lady director, telling her how he should play the role. Right then I thought, "Uh-oh, what have I done?" Here I was, giving him his only chance to play Broadway because I thought he was a friend, yet I'd later receive a nasty letter when he heard I had thrown a party without inviting him. I never realized he was that small.

Of course, one of my true friends was Bob Hope. He saw the

show with Dolores and then walked onstage and did a fifteen-
minute routine while the entire cast looked on. That was a memorable night. It had nothing to do with Bob stealing the limelight.
It was about giving. This was a compliment to me and, since everyone knew about our professional relationship, an added bonus for
the audience. He was such a darling, generous man. Unfortunately, the notices for the production itself had been less than
charitable. They were so bad, some of my friends in the press had
tried to protect me—the *New York Times* review appeared in the
financial section.

To be honest, the matinée that the critics attended was simply
awful. The audience was full of old hairpins—little old ladies
with blue hair who were either half asleep or half dead—while
an old, old stagehand guaranteed I'd never forget that horrible
performance. It was his job to ensure my dress didn't get caught
in the wheels of the little train that first transported me onstage.
Well, he didn't do his job and I got caught in the wheels during
my grand entrance. Ignorant of the mechanics, I wanted them to
stop, but they couldn't. Everything was operated down in the
bowels of the theater. Fortunately, one of the dancers untangled
me while I said my opening lines, but I was a broken woman.
God knows what the rest of the show was like. I managed to forget long ago.

On the actual opening night, while I stood in the wings, that
aforementioned stagehand chose to tell me how he'd been
around since the days of George M. Cohan. Nervous as hell, trying to concentrate, scared I wouldn't remember a single line, I

was treated to the old asshole's entire history, including every detail of how great he was . . . *Shut up!* I didn't know how to protect myself from people like that. "Please be quiet, I'm trying to think." The silly bastard went on and on and on. Still, as far as I was concerned I did a good job, playing everything straight and never once inserting a laugh. I had been properly cast—Dolly is supposed to be a redheaded Irishwoman—and I performed the part with spirit and softness. Then, when my three months were up, I was replaced by the woman for whom the show had been written, the woman who had turned it down in the first place: Ethel Merman. She was another good friend.

It was in May 1971 that I made my debut as a piano soloist, adopting the virtuoso pseudonym Dame Illya Dillya. In my mid-fifties, I at last had a public outlet for all the private practice, a means of fulfilling some of the failed dreams of my music school years. And, like so many other things relating to my career, it came about by happy accident. For the longest time, I had played the Holiday House just outside Pittsburgh—a big nightclub with a large orchestra, serving good food. Like clockwork, I was there every autumn when the women's bowling teams had their annual competition. Well, one morning in my bedroom at home, I received a call from someone representing the Pittsburgh Pops, asking whether I'd do a show for them. Thinking music and symphony I said, "Oh, I'll play a little Bach and a little Beethoven. I'd *love* that!" There was silence on the other end of the phone while the guy regained consciousness. He didn't let on that he only wanted my comedy act. It became my first symphony performance. If this negotiation had been handled by anyone else—an agent or a manager—I would have never enjoyed ten wonderful years of concert work.

I'm dedicated to culture. I honestly believe there's absolutely nothing wrong about going to bed with a good book . . . or a friend who's read one.

After the first concert had been arranged I spent four months practicing every day, often with Bob Alberti, an NBC musician who occasionally filled in for pianist Ross Tompkins on *The Tonight Show*. Bob, who also served as Bob Hope's musical director, was a dear friend, although he informed me that, due to Warde's interfering presence, he could never be *my* musical director. Sitting at back-to-back pianos, Alberti would play the orchestral parts while I learned when and where to come in. That was my coaching. It might have been a bold move on my part—I would be performing without any sort of safety net—yet, since no one expected me to play, audiences would be in for quite a surprise.

Again, I didn't think about this too much. I'm at my happiest onstage and I always look forward to a performance. I'm totally involved, all alone except for a solitary spotlight. So, I went with my gut instinct. Soloing on piano was a major thrill, even though I never felt comfortable. I'm comfortable with standup work. I never did enough piano concerts to feel free and avoid being a nervous wreck. My hands would always be ice cold and I'd feel breathless, but I had to go on. It was a challenge, and I accepted that challenge and did my best. That's all anyone can do.

A Dame and a Drunk

When she started to play, Steinway himself came down personally and rubbed his name off the piano.

—Bob Hope

I am not a concert pianist, and neither was Victor Borge, but he *could* have been. I couldn't. I didn't have that deeper talent: the synapse between my brain cells and the tips of my fingers. What I did have, thanks to all those years of practice, was a wonderful facility. I could play delicately and I could play fast, and that made me sound really good. I was never terrific at playing big pieces with intricate chords, but my agility got me through. Some of my performances were great, others were less than great, but I always worked real hard. It's a tough discipline when you're aware that one bum note spells trouble, but if I fouled up I'd look at the audience and, referring to the orchestra members, say, "They've got music." As a comic I could get by with that, whereas a concert artist would have to keep going.

The bookings used to last anywhere from a week to three weeks, and, wherever I was, I always had to have a piano on which to practice. However, as more and more of my bookings became one-nighters there was no way to practice, and this lessened my facility. It was then that I let the concert work fade away. Through March 1982, I sustained a career by performing with a hundred symphony orchestras all over the United States and Canada, and I'm *really* proud of that.

The first half of the show always comprised a performance by the symphony before I'd be announced in the style of the old NBC Sunday night concerts: "The orchestra is tuning and back-

stage the excitement is building. Dame Illya Dillya has just returned from a triumphal tour of Butte, Montana . . ." Immediately the audience got the picture—they were in for something,
they just didn't know what. In hushed, reverential tones the announcer would then say, "Ladies and gentlemen, Dame Illya
Dillya!" and I would *sweep* onstage to much applause in my blue
outfit and white fur. The Michael Travis coat and sleeveless
Marusha dress are now in the Allen County Museum in Lima,
Ohio, while a sleeved copy of the dress is in the Smithsonian—
this version, designed by Omar, was wider around the waist to accommodate my eating . . . plus a little gin. The outfit weighed
fifty pounds and it got tighter and tighter. I wasn't used to that. I
normally wore loose clothes to cover up and give the illusion of
a bad figure, but I reached the point where it wasn't an illusion.

Seating myself at the piano, I first had to deal with three-
quarter-length white gloves, majestically peeling one off my left
hand and tossing it onto the floor before trying to do the same
with the other which was about ten feet long. Pulling on this
endless glove, I'd look quite annoyed, especially when it appeared
to be attached to my underwear, but finally I'd unravel the damned
thing and again toss it onto the floor. Now I'd look at the audience and they'd look at me, wondering what the hell might happen next. Quickly, I'd toss the white fur to the ground and then,
facing the conductor with my back to the audience, unzip my
coat all the way down so that he had a visible fit, presumably
shocked by my naked body.

So far, not a word had been spoken—it was pure pantomime . . .
and pretense. Turning around, I'd step out of the coat *fully dressed*

and get ready to play. But first I had to get rid of the clothes that were all over the floor, so I'd look to the wings and clap my hands, and two stretcher-bearers would rush towards me from the other end of the stage. Everything was wrong. Regardless, these men would carefully arrange the clothes like a body on a stretcher and make their exit. At last I was ready for my grand performance . . . except there was no bench for me to sit on. I'd therefore take the concert master's chair and leave him standing. He'd then take somebody else's chair, that person would take somebody else's, and this would continue all the way to the back of the violin section. The last violinist, who had to be awakened, would fetch the piano bench from backstage, adjust it for himself, and struggle with me before handing it over. There was a unique charm to seeing seemingly stuffy musicians participate in broad comedy.

Written mostly by me, this silent twelve-minute routine was all about incompetence despite pretensions of grandeur, and it ended with me stepping *over* the bench, gown and all, before sitting down. Wearing a tiara with a feather, I'd bow to the conductor and he'd bow back, but he wouldn't commence the first musical piece. Again, I'd bow and he would bow back, and now I'd look at the audience, demanding a laugh like Oliver Hardy did when he glanced into the camera. Suddenly remembering where we were and what we were supposed to be doing, the conductor and I would bow a final time and the concert would begin. During the musical prologue, I'd dust the piano, check the score, and look at the audience through my binoculars—it was a *long* preamble—before straightening up and launching into the first movement of Beethoven's Piano Concerto No. 1. Once I was into the music, I was serious, and many in the audience were more than a little surprised. They had probably been wondering if I would ever really play, and some would be convinced that my performance was on tape.

For me this was a whole new act and a whole new persona in front of a whole new group of people; no Fang, no ugly jokes. It was a send-up of the classical world, pure and simple, and it basically wrote itself along with some help from Gene Perret. I said, "I need some Beethoven jokes," and he came up with "Beethoven and I both had the same hairdo. He moved fifty-six times because he was a *terrible* housekeeper . . . and he had *horrible* body odor."

When introducing *Ave Maria*, which is really Bach's *First Prelude*, I'd remark, "Chuck Gounod heard it and said, 'There's no melody.' So, he wrote a melody." I'd then play it, and before I performed the Bach *Inventions* I would joke about the composer's name and his twenty offspring: "Bach's wife didn't call him Johann, she called him 'Yo-Yo.' He had the first piano bench that opened out into a bed, and when the music stopped Mrs. Bach broke out in a cold sweat . . . Twenty kids! Of *course* she was overworked. One day while doing the laundry, she told Yo-Yo, 'You've got to take some of these kids off my hands.' She had a terrible diaper rash on her head as she'd wrapped it in a wet diaper . . ."

By writing these lines I was transforming the Bachs into the Bickersons. It was a lively show, and I was onstage just under an hour, ending with two straight musical numbers that I sang as a lyric soprano, losing my top notes with every passing hour: "The

Ladies Who Lunch" from Stephen Sondheim's *Company*, and Jerry Herman's "Before the Parade Passes By" from *Hello, Dolly!*

> *"I've gotta get in step while there's still time left*
> *I'm ready to move out in front*
> *Life without life has no reason or rhyme left"*

"Before the Parade Passes By" was a wonderful closer because I was already getting up there in years. It personified me, and it also embodied my attitude so well that I included it in my regular standup act. Still, that didn't stop certain people from getting in the way. One time, at Harrah's in Lake Tahoe, I was rehearsing the number with a wonderful big band—when they still had big bands—and right in the middle, Warde insisted I was singing something wrong. I wasn't. *He* was wrong, but he presented himself as the big musical know-it-all, the bandleader unfortunately didn't object, and my husband's interruption served to close down the rehearsal. I bet him $150 that I was right and I won the bet—Christ, I'd performed that number for three months on Broadway. Still, you don't have to be Einstein to figure out what was going on inside Warde's head. Jealous of my success, he felt the need to assert himself by way of emphasizing his own talent and expertise, and he did so in some truly awful ways.

Performing at the Beverly Hills Casino in Kentucky, across the river from Cincinnati, I wanted to insert another new number into my show, yet it was Warde who rehearsed it with the band. My rehearsal! That meant I had to go onstage without rehearsing and try to sing a new number. Of course, just as at Harrah's, I should have told him to butt the hell out of my affairs, but I didn't have the stomach for a confrontation. Then, on my closing night at the Beverly Hills Casino, he got totally drunk and kept buying me evening bags from the gift shop. Total madness. Warde was the most adorable man when sober, sweet to children and animals and old ladies, but when he got drunk he was really mean, especially to other people with whom he felt obliged to create a scene.

The night before I was due to perform with the Cincinnati Symphony Orchestra I had a standup gig at the highbrow Republican Club in Indianapolis. It was the most chic of all WASP venues. Warde and I were given the star suite and full VIP treatment, but throughout that show he was at the bar. Consequently, when a woman approached him and asked, "Are you connected with Phyllis Diller?" he replied, "Yes, I fuck her every night." He could say that again. He was screwing my mind as well as my career. Just so my husband had something to do I'd asked him to rehearse the band, but later I was informed that, had the musicians not harbored a great deal of love for me, they would have never performed.

After the show, there was no food available at the club, so the chef asked us what we wanted. A hamburger or a bowl of soup would have been fine with me. But no, my big-shot husband ordered the two of us Baked Alaska, which has to be served flaming and is ordinarily prepared for a larger group of people. I could have *died*. Still, I'm not through with this story. The next day we traveled by limo to Cincinnati alongside my secretary, Corinne, and my stand-in, Molly, who doubled as my helper. Warde looked terribly important in his Richard Burton–style mink coat, yet when we arrived he realized that he had forgotten the music for my symphony performance. It was all in one case, and it had to be driven from Indianapolis in time for the show. I was furious. He was drunk that entire day, and when he tried to put in his two cents' worth during rehearsals the orchestra librarian snapped, "Get rid of this guy or I quit." A mink draped over the shoulders didn't impress the folks of Ohio.

A short time later, Warde and I were sitting in a Las Vegas restaurant with my dear friend Marc London. We were in a booth, the champagne was in a bucket of ice, and a sweet old waiter brought three glasses which Warde complained weren't the right shape. Then, when the waiter took them back and returned with flutes, Warde said, "They aren't chilled." Okay, so now the waiter removed the flutes and returned with ones that were chilled, at which point, having already made a complete ass of himself, Warde got up and knocked over the ice bucket. It was like something out of a bad movie. (And believe me, I've made a few of *them*.) Beforehand, aware of how drunk Warde already was, I'd asked Marc to drive us to the restaurant and Warde wouldn't let him. Now, with even more booze inside him, I was scared he would kill us on the way home. This is what it was like to live with a man who was pretty smashed every night. Smashed because he wasn't working.

I went into a clothes store one day and the lady said, "Madam, you have got to try this dress on. It is so sexy, it will give your husband ideas." I said, "What, does a brain come with it?"

Marc London was in a revue that I wrote and starred in at the Tropicana. *Hellzapoppin'* was on Broadway at the time, it was about to close, and my show was in the same mould, featuring a singing group, a marvelous piano team comprised of twins Mark & Clark, and an orchestra led by Peter Daniels, as well as Pat McCormack and myself in a skit where he was a ventriloquist and I was his dummy. It was a darling show, produced and directed by Joe Layton, and it cost me a fortune. My manager, Roy Gerber, was supposed to make the right connection and get it to Broadway, but he didn't make a move. He didn't make one lousy phone call. Back then the Tropicana wasn't a hotel, it was just a gambling and entertainment venue, located all alone at the very end of the strip. It was a very bad investment, but that wasn't the only problem.

Since I always tried to work Warde into anything I did, he had a comic role as a head waiter. Nevertheless, before opening night he spent the entire day getting drunk. There was a realtor who'd helped me buy two homes—she was always after me—and Warde took her to look at houses throughout that afternoon. Everywhere they visited he would say, "I'd like a drink," and if the people offered him water, he would say, "No, vodka." We were staying at the house of Artie Shaw and Betty Grable, and Warde returned there and passed out on the bed while the show was going on, so Joe Layton had to fill in for him. Imagine! On *opening night*. That was it. I threw Warde out of the show and out of my life. I moved into the Tropicana and he stayed for quite a while in Artie's house—whenever Marc and I played tennis on one of the Tropicana's indoor courts after the show, Warde would watch us from the balcony. That was the second time we parted. And then I took him back. I was so crazy about the man, yet every time I had an opening night he would do something awful. Why, oh *why*, did I think his behavior would ever change?

Eventually, there were limo companies that refused my business because Warde had obviously given them hell. It was, in essence, like *A Star Is Born*. In the beginning, having done Broadway and London and appeared in his own show, he thought he was a star. He even had his own fan club, but I was on the rise and I was hot, so before long all of the calls were for me. I made people hire him, but finally they wouldn't. He had nothing to do, and it got worse. I couldn't even get him to open for me. After all, Warde Donovan wasn't a name like others who had opened for me, like singers Enzo Stuarti and Jerry Vale, so he was reduced to doing my announcements. And even then there were many, many times when he didn't show up. I couldn't depend on him. I'd have to make the announcements myself and then walk on-stage with a broken heart. What's more, when Warde did make the announcements, they kept getting longer and longer in order to heighten his own importance. All he really had to do was say, "Here she is, Phyllis Diller," but he turned it into *his* part of the show.

Finally, one night in San Francisco, he went too far, ruining a performance by leaving his microphone *on* in the noisy back-stage area. The magician Mercer Helms was opening for me and I could hear his pigeons cooing the entire time. That was the last straw. The marriage had lasted almost ten years, and this would be our third and final separation. I doubt that Warde's forgetfulness was due to passive aggression. It was probably due to his fall out of that second-story window. However, the time arrived when a friend of his, an old movie actress named Marta Linden, said, "I don't know how you stand it, Phyllis," and by now I couldn't. The year was 1975. I filed for divorce that February.

Following our split, I would occasionally run into Warde around the neighborhood and he'd always want me to join him for a drink, even after he'd remarried. He would have done anything to get back with me, regardless of the situation, but I was no longer interested and I couldn't be tempted. In the words of "Before the Parade Passes By," I wanted to "feel my heart coming alive again," and I had the goods to do it. After all, I was blessed with health, wealth, fascinating work, fabulous friends, and the love of my kids. And what's more, I also had something new to feel positive about: my *good looks* . . . try not to laugh.

Ten

A CHANGE OF FACE

My mother said, "You have inner beauty," and I said, "Well, why was I born wrong-side-out?"

I t was during the early years of my career, while performing at Mister Kelly's in Chicago, that I met *Playboy* boss Hugh Hefner. Soon afterwards I appeared on his show *Playboy After Dark*, and I also attended parties at the seventy-room Playboy Mansion located on North State Parkway, in the city's ritzy Gold Coast district, where a brass plate on the front door bore the Latin inscription *Si Non Oscillas, Noli Tintinnare*—If You Don't Swing, Don't Ring. *Oh, baby.*

As a constant visitor to Chicago, I was a regular at the Mansion—one time, when I wanted to go swimming in the Grotto, Hef loaned me a swimsuit that made me realize some of his chicks *weren't* perfect. Still, the two of us enjoyed a friendship on a whole different level. I wasn't one of the airheads, and like him I was also a big jazz freak. But then, during the late sixties, I was asked to pose nude for the magazine, and although more than a little surprised, I agreed. I mean, how often would this kind of request come *my* way? I immediately knew what the idea was. And I'd subsequently be more than aware why it didn't work.

The mag had just done a comic shoot with Mama Cass, the oversized former singer in the Mamas & the Papas. Onstage, meanwhile, I was referring to myself as chest-less: "the only woman in America with two backs. Nobody knows whether I'm coming or going." Assuming I was skinny, the *Playboy* brass reasoned it made perfect sense to follow Cass with Diller. Ugly, bony, scrawny is what they were after, but while I certainly matched the first requirement and also had skinny limbs, the editors didn't realize I dressed specifically to hide my large tits—with Raglan sleeves, you don't have breasts. Back then, before I had a reduction, I was a size 38D—*grapefruits*—and all this became very apparent when I stepped out of my clothes and in front of the cameras. It wasn't what they wanted at all.

I convinced everyone I was flat. I was 38D. I had nursed the world.

The shoot went ahead but the photos were never used, and a short while later they tried again. This time around, the lights blew. As usual, they played beautiful music and gave me champagne . . . the lights still blew. *Everything* blew. For me, posing nude was not such a big deal. Okay, I was a bit self-conscious, but having been around showbiz dressing rooms for quite a while and seen boys and girls run past each other in various states of undress and *deshabillé*—not to mention all those other *habillés*—I'd lost any feelings of shyness. After all, whenever you perform you are naked in front of the audience . . . metaphorically speaking. That's what they love about it. If you're going to stop and worry about that, you're never going to make an entrance.

My Playtex Living Bra died . . . of starvation. I've turned many a head in my day, and a few stomachs. I never made Who's Who *but I'm featured in* What's That?

Back in clothes, I continued to make numerous appearances before the TV cameras, including an August 1971 episode of *The Sonny and Cher Comedy Hour* in which I performed a witchy, witchy role in some campy skit. Once again, the lighting evidently wasn't too great, because when I watched that broadcast I was shocked by the skin hanging under my chin. I had never noticed it before, and the terrible bags under my eyes were also distressing. I assumed all this was a sign of debauchery, but it wasn't. It was fat. In fact, when I thought back, I'd had this problem in college, so it wasn't even due to age. It was a hereditary fat thing. I had never noticed any of this in my mirror. Now I was horrified.

After watching the show, I went straight to the phone and called a dermatologist: "Doctor, I want to have my face fixed. To whom do I go?" He said, "Dr. Franklin Ashley." Head of cosmetic surgery at UCLA, Dr. Ashley was *the* plastic surgeon of the world, catering to all the stars, from Ann-Margret to John Wayne. No doubt about it, Ashley was the man for me, and if he was going to take care of the fat under my eyes and chin then he might as well go ahead and fix the crooked, pointy nose that had bothered me all my life.

I had to do something. I was so wrinkled, I could screw my hats on. And talk about ugly—my own Ouija board told me to go to hell. One night, a peeping Tom threw up on my windowsill.

As things turned out, when I went in that first time I had the complete neck-nose-eyes job, as well as a lift, and Dr. Ashley's work was amazing. He really tightened everything . . . with *rope*. It was a whole new me, a whole new face. I'd never asked Dr. Ashley to change the shape of my nose, I had just wanted it to be un-broken. He, however, knew how it should and could look. In true Driver tradition it was too long, and so Ashley took it upon himself to give me a new, perfect nose by moving, bobbing, and reshaping it.

When I woke up the day after the operation, I had just one lit-tle slit of an eye. Remember, I'd had the works. Since my nose was packed to prevent it from becoming crooked again I breathed through my mouth and I was *barely alive*. This was all in the name of making me happy. Then, when the nurses took my bandages off, I was a mess; a mass of purples that would turn to greens, reds, oranges, browns, and back to purples. In accordance with Dr. Ashley's prior warning, it was the equivalent of being involved in a head-on car crash and I looked like the Bride of

Frankenstein . . . well, not that good. Still, I never had doubts or questions. Everything was half-full, not half-empty. I believed in magic, the magic came through, and once I had healed, the result was all I could have hoped for. I loved it. I'd been given a pretty face.

My dear, close friend, the publicist Frank Liberman, had been dead against all this. Aware that my old face had been my fortune, he was sure that making it look better would ruin my career. Boy, how *wrong* could he be? I was determined to follow my gut feeling without taking anybody's advice. I never gave a thought as to how I'd keep joking about being ugly, and as time has revealed, I didn't have to. The ugly jokes would remain a part of my act because my image was already so well established. Audiences had bought into it because, facially at least, it had been the truth, and for them it would continue to be the truth.

Of course, it caused a sensation when I attended parties with the stitches sticking out of my face and a pair of glasses taped to my forehead so that they wouldn't sit on my fragile new nose. I didn't do it for effect, that's just the way I am. It meant nothing to me. "What are you doing Thursday?" "Oh, I'm having a face-lift." Now everyone had a chance to get a close-up look at the real thing and they were fascinated—"My *God,* is that the way it's *done?*" Among the people who said this were those who, despite already having had surgery themselves, pretended they hadn't. And in several cases, the work was so obvious their surgeon should have signed it.

Frank Liberman still thought I shouldn't talk about my own surgery, but again he was wrong, and he's the first to admit it. I lived off the topic for years, discussing it on talk shows and speaking about it at public events. It was the main subject. I was willing to talk and everyone was interested because I knew all the answers. What's more, I was able to work it into my act. This was a whole new area for me to explore.

I told Fang, "I'm gonna have my face lifted," and he said, "Who the hell would steal it?"

A lot of people would have agreed with Frank that it was a bad idea to go public about the cosmetic surgery, but turning this on its head worked completely to my advantage. My mother used to quote a line from the Bible: "We know that all things work together for good for those who love God, to those who are called according to his purpose." My edited version is: "All things work together for good for those who love," and I believe it. I am a loving person and that's why things work. It's karma.

Having spent so many years doing work, work, work, I'd started to get a little slipshod about the way I dressed. My feet had also been giving me hell, so I was wearing flat shoes, and, all in all, my great love of fashion had given way to me being a little sloppy, not even taking great pains with the makeup. After the face-lift, however, *boom*. It was a whole new attitude, a whole new me, taking great care of my clothes and makeup now that I had something to work with. I wanted to make the face as pretty as possible because at last it was something to be proud of. *Narcissus*. It was really nice.

Now that I'd started the ball rolling, there was no stopping me. I underwent another fourteen surgical procedures over the next fifteen years, and each time it resulted from my being shocked by what I saw beforehand. On one occasion I was sitting in a TV studio, someone took a Polaroid of me, and when I saw the result I thought I was looking at a beached whale. Now, most people who feel as depressed as I did might consider a diet to be the obvious solution, but I'm a foodie. I had been on diets before. One of them required me to avoid all liquor for three months, and I did turn into a wonderfully skinny broad, but *oh* God. A life on the stage is full of tension. You keep visiting new places and encountering new people, so you're never fully relaxed, and when your name is on the marquee, you worry whether the business is going to be good or bad. It's all about stress. And after the show, a drink is a fast way to relax.

Therefore, with a diet nowhere on my radar screen, I opted to have a breast reduction, lift, and tummy tuck, and afterwards my body looked fabulous . . . for a few minutes. The fat came back right away. What a waste of time, although without the surgery I probably would have ended up twice as fat. Now, *that's* a truly horrible thought. I wouldn't want to have anybody slit *my* girdle open and watch me spread to death.

My plastic surgeon took one look at me and wanted to add a tail. He said my face looked like a bouquet of elbows.

There isn't a female comic who doesn't want to be a great beauty. The four top comediennes of the seventies all went for surgery: Joan Rivers, Carol Burnett, Totie Fields, and me. The other surgeries I had included teeth straightening and bonding, an eyeliner tattoo that quickly wore off, and having a tiny amount of fat taken from my navel area and shot into wrinkles around my mouth. This got rid of the vertical lines that afflict all really old dames.

The American Academy of Cosmetic Surgery subsequently presented me with an award for "the tremendous breakthrough in acceptance for our field, when she was the first person to have the courage to proclaim her surgery and show her results publicly." That was the topper. The subject had always been treated like an abortion; something you whispered about, something that was referred to in magazines by way of dotted lines, never about a real person. Well, I screwed all that. I was a walking billboard for plastic surgery and I was a good one because I never looked like I'd had anything done. The doctors would call *me* to ask if I fancied having some more work, and they'd offer it for nothing in return for all the publicity. The most generous was Dr. Michael Elam, a young guy with movie-star good looks who gave me a free forehead lift, a chemical peel, cheek implants, another eye job, and even another nose job after I fell and broke it again. I tripped over some luggage on my way to the pot and landed flat on my face—every hotel room is different, but I should have known better than to leave a packed suitcase in the middle of the floor.

When I die, God won't know me. There are no two parts of my body the same age. If I have one more face-lift, it'll be cesarean. My face has been pulled up more times than Bill Clinton's pants.

The peel didn't hurt until they ripped off the skin. Acid was applied overnight, and the next morning the surgeon fiddled around with my face before suddenly *rrriiippp!* Oh my God, that was painful, if only for a moment. And I must say, for a while my skin was as smooth as a baby's butt. What's more, all the freckles were removed, so for the first time in my life I had smooth, *spotless* skin. The first layer was gone altogether and now I was onto the second layer—it was like undergoing a controlled burn.

I always had wonderful work and the result was that I never, ever looked like I'd undergone surgery. Okay, so people probably noticed I had a brand new face, but what the heck? Regardless of your age, if the work is done properly it'll make you look ten years younger. And after quite a few surgeries nothing was bothering me. I had a look that I could live with, so I never had any more done despite the doctors continuing to follow me around, saying, "Here's what you need. Here's what you've got to have done." I always fought them off, most often about smoothing my hands. That would have amounted to injecting fat, yet all it does is cover your blue blood.

The woman next door had her nose fixed and now her mouth won't work. She said, "I've found this divine new plastic surgeon," and I said, "Well, I don't know how divine he is, but I'm sure he's new." She said, "I just love him, he's marvelous, and he's very cheap." I said, "I can tell you something else about him; he's left-handed."

I underwent fifteen different procedures, but I never overdid anything. Not for me the Chinese eyes or the permanently startled expression. Many women look like they're wearing a mask, and when men get into it things can turn really nasty. Some look just plain strange. Men should allow themselves to age naturally because it's more acceptable in their case. Age wears well on them. It's masculine to be craggy and rugged, and women love mileage on a man. All that men should ever have corrected are the eye bags, above and below, and the waffle: the hanging neck and sagging chin line. Dr. Ashley used to *beg* me to persuade Ronnie Reagan to let him fix his neck.

Many people much younger than I are playing around with their faces and it makes them look so unreal. Some of them are beautiful women in their early twenties—they get hooked and then they're in trouble. You can only stretch skin so far. That's why I am through with cosmetic surgery. And besides, when you reach my age, there's not a whole lot to gain from looking ten years younger.

It was that first surgery which made the major difference, and thereafter it was really just a case of fine-tuning. No longer frightened when I saw myself on TV, I felt far more comfortable about going before the cameras, and that was fortunate because my schedule was loaded with television work. During the seventies and eighties this included appearances on *Rowan & Martin's Laugh-In*, *The Carol Burnett Show*, *The Flip Wilson Show*, *The Muppet Show*, *CHiPS*, *The Love Boat*, a bunch of talk shows, and, best of all, the *Dean Martin Celebrity Roasts*. What a blast those were.

Filmed at the MGM Grand in Las Vegas, Dino's NBC specials featured many of the biggest names in the business; an incredible collection, ranging from Orson Welles, Jimmy Stewart, Lucille

Ball, Bob Hope, Sammy Davis, Jr., and Frank Sinatra to Muhammad Ali, Ronald Reagan, Telly Savalas, George Burns, John Wayne, and the original roaster, Don Rickles. Oh, I *love* Don Rickles. Talk about mock hostility. He'd have everyone falling about. There was a live audience, real booze, and those glasses weren't filled with colored water, baby. Each one-hour show took a couple of hours to tape and there'd be plenty of genuine laughs, but the whole thing was also very tiring—we were being stared at for two hours, so there could be no nose-picking. It was a tense situation. Everyone wanted to be funny, no one wanted to be the lame duck.

My fan club broke up today. The guy died.

Most people who appeared on the *Celebrity Roasts* were at the top of their game, and they and numerous others made an indelible impression on me. They were the *crème de la crème* and I have good memories of them all: Robert Mitchum, Richard Burton, Jack Benny, Bette Davis, Dolly Parton, Dudley Moore, Liberace, and Jack Lemmon, to name just a few. I'd previously met Jack at a party thrown for Lady Sassoon, the widow and former nurse of international financier Sir Victor Sassoon. She was one of those people whose birthday parties last all year and are celebrated around the world, in various towns and countries. Well, Jack was a fabulous pianist, and the two of us sat down at the grand piano and spent the entire night playing jazz together. That was one of the high points of my entire life.

Bob Mitchum, meanwhile, was a close neighbor and even

closer friend; an adorable man and wonderful guest. He'd really open up at parties, regaling everyone with stories about his past, and it was fascinating, like listening to a live soap opera. He had been to jail thirty-seven times and had even worked on a chain gang. That man had balls. The first party I had at my house, in about 1966, was a sit-down for 150 people, and in every huge goblet of water was a goldfish. Obviously that was a joke and a party favor, but Mitchum *drank* his. What a nut. He was so precious, I adored him, and the two of us were regulars in each other's homes.

Another good friend and great party guest was George Burns, who would go into his old act, joking and singing without being asked. It was only natural for us to entertain one another—that happened automatically, especially when a bunch of comics got together. Some would try to outdo others, not least the guys, and, all in all, we'd have a wonderful time. It was about camaraderie and sharing in what we did best; entertaining people, making them laugh. And it was also about enjoying the perks of our profession. One minute, I was meeting Elvis Presley—we just stared at one another and had nothing to say—and the next, I was mixing with Brit royals.

In May 1974, I attended the 100th Kentucky Derby, where the guests of honor were Princess Margaret and Tony Snowdon. A very exclusive reception took place after the race—it was standing-room only—and I somehow ended up talking to them in the center of the room without being able to understand a word they said. Their accents were *so* exaggerated. Margaret only came up to my shoulders—she was a short little broad—and for a half-hour we just stood there, trying to communicate. I had to keep asking what they were saying. It was embarrassing. I couldn't walk away and nobody approached us.

Several years later, during the early eighties, I appeared in a Bob Hope TV special filmed at a London theater where Prince Philip was seated in the box closest to the stage. Debbie Reynolds, Brooke Shields, and Bernadette Peters were also in the show, and afterwards, when we were introduced to Philip onstage, he turned to me and said, "You're the American Boy George." That was his idea of a compliment. I'm sure he was referring to my strange outfits . . . at least, I hope he was.

Since divorcing Warde I'd been footloose and fancy-free, happy to do my thing without having a man insult me, abuse me, or act like a noose around my neck. But then, one night in 1985, I met the love of my life. His name was Robert P. Hastings and he was the cofounder of one of the world's largest and most prestigious law firms, Paul, Hastings, Janofsky & Walker. Bob was introduced to me by Jeffie Pike, the daughter of artist Marion Pike, who said, "Boy, do I have a guy for you," and was she ever right.

After graduating Yale, where he was captain of the tennis team, Bob had studied law at Harvard and then formed the Los Angeles firm of Paul, Hastings & Edmonds in 1946 with friends Lee Paul and Warner Edmonds. Five years later, following Edmonds' departure to set up a practice in Santa Barbara, Bob and Lee were joined by fellow Harvard graduate Leonard Janofsky, before tax attorney Charles Walker completed the partnership in

1962. This solidified a company that, by the time I met Bob, had offices in L.A., Orange County, San Francisco, Atlanta, Washington, D.C., Stamford, and New York City. A couple of years later it would also have the first American law office in Japan.

An Anglophile and an authority on Winston Churchill, Bob Hastings was the most fabulous gentleman; a refined, immaculately dressed *bon viveur* who knocked me out from the moment we first set eyes on each other at his home in Pasadena, a few miles northeast of Los Angeles. Jeffie and her husband had arranged to meet me there, and after a while they left us alone.

Well, that was it. *Wow!* Jeffie had done a real good job of predicting chemistry between two people. Bob and I had *everything* in common—emotionally, philosophically, you name it—and we laughed at the same things in the same way. He was an incredibly passionate man, interested in all around him, and his sweetness towards everyone was just one of the things I greatly admired. I'd admire that in anyone, and boy, he had it to the nth degree.

I was sixty-eight when we met, Bob was seventy-five, and having been a great beauty in his youth he still had that look of intelligence and authority. His wife had been dead for eight years and every woman in Pasadena was after him, yet I offered something they didn't have: *fun*. Bob loved to hear me play the piano and he absolutely adored my standup work—he had a fabulous sense of humor, and he thought that what I did was just miraculous. Every time he saw a show, you'd think he had never seen it before. That man was something else. And since the two of us got on so well, we had a great time living apart together.

Every weekend he would travel from his firm's downtown office to my home, and we'd divide our time between here and his place because we both loved to entertain. What's more, at the very start of our great romance, he took me on a weekend trip to the beautiful San Ysidro Ranch in Santa Barbara, where he'd managed to reserve the Kennedy Cottage in which JFK and Jackie had spent their honeymoon back in 1953. For me this was like our own honeymoon and I adored every minute. We each brought our tennis rackets—I think Bob's was the old wooden one that he had used at Yale, which I insisted was a snowshoe—and after hitting a few shots across the court, I realized we must *never* play tennis, because I would have beaten the crap out of him. . . . Always make your man feel like a winner.

After that weekend, he wanted to take me on trips all the time, but I balked. As a comic who had spent so much time on the road, my trip was being at home. However, this was also a period when I performed on numerous cruise ships, so we did still travel a lot together. Hired by many of the top cruise companies, I always had a wonderful deal—I'd be provided with a fantastic suite and, since the ship invariably had an orchestra, I didn't need to bring my own musicians and could therefore offer guests a terrific free cruise. For Bob and I this amounted to a lot of time spent playing Diller Gin, which is my customized version of the traditional card game. Once you play it, you're hooked, and Bob was hooked.

This guy had lived an upscale Pasadena life with a society wife who mixed with friends at the exclusive Valley Hunt Club and had almost daily social lunches at the nearby Annandale Golf Club. At home they, of course, had a housekeeper, and since the kitchen was pretty small he had never ventured in there. My kitchen, on the other hand, is the heart of the house: a warm, bright-red, antique-filled sitting room. Every room in my house is a sitting room, be it my office, my bedroom, the guest rooms, the Coolidge-style porch, or the kitchen. Well, when Bob lived with me we'd spend a fair amount of time in that kitchen, and he always insisted on washing the dishes. To him this was *fascinating*. Used to working until two or three in the morning, I'm a late sleeper; so on Sunday mornings he would always be up earlier, reading the paper in the kitchen while getting his own breakfast. Since he'd never had the chance to do this before, it was a thrilling new experience; a graduate of Harvard and Yale, a leading authority on Churchill, who was now deriving major pleasure from some of life's simplest chores. Not that these were the only source.

Old folks, you see, know all about having fun, even if they have to use a little more imagination, and I had one particular peignoir that was Bob's favorite. It was black over nudity, and I'd wear it while dancing to music. Thank God it was not totally see-through. It was shadowy see-through, so he could just about tell somebody was in there.

The best contraceptive for old people is nudity . . . And condoms for old guys are called software. They're now selling condoms right out in the open, up at the cash register. I always order three and say, "Fill 'em up . . . with M&M's."

I admired everything about my new partner. He and his associates were the total opposite of everyone I knew. Bob would
take me to events involving Paul, Hastings, Janofsky & Walker,
and I was out of mind, awed by these people's knowledge and intelligence. I was impressed by him, he was impressed by me, and
we had this great relationship because, although we were from
totally different worlds, we did complement each other perfectly.
I've always admired intelligence, so I was totally at home with
Bob and his colleagues. And since he had a great sense of humor,
he also loved and admired what I did. It was the ideal melding of
two personalities, and he was the light of my life.

Being with Bob really elevated me, energized me, and encour-
aged me to expand my horizons; so it was probably no coincidence that, shortly after embarking on our relationship, I began
painting for pleasure—exploiting an ability that I'd been aware
of since childhood but had never pursued. Constantly on the
road, I rarely had the time or the space to paint, yet all this
changed in 1986 when I was at Harrah's in Reno, staying in a
magnificent penthouse suite; entrance hall, big bedroom, big
guest bedroom, big dining room. Suddenly I found myself with
the space to inadvertently launch a career that would see my artwork displayed in galleries across the United States and, in some
cases, sell for thousands of dollars.

You see, I'm fast in terms of everything I do, so there was no
way I'd be sitting down to do just one painting. I started with wa-
tercolors and, as I went from one canvas to the next, I was able
to let the results dry on the beds in the guest room as well as on

the dining-room table. There was a piano in the living room, but I didn't have the need or the inclination to practice anymore. So, with some spare hours on my hands, the space in that Harrah's suite inspired me to paint, and every time I returned there I took the necessary tools.

Then, while attending a benefit in Oklahoma City where Willie Nelson was performing, I gave the organizers a painting they could auction and an art collector bought it for $5,000. I thought, "Ka-ching!" It was those good old dollar signs, baby. Forget what I've earned throughout my career—I *always* need the money. When I was a little kid and Mother handed me a carbonated drink, she'd say, "Get the bubbles, that's the money." It was ingrained in me. So, I started painting and very quickly found myself enjoying it and making a lot of sales.

Less than great when it came to abstract art, I didn't want to try to fool anybody. Faces were my thing. I'd paint them easily and paint them best. I never studied the art form or intellectualized it. I just enjoyed making choices about what colors to use and whether or not the subject should wear a hat. I was having a *ball*. And as I'd always been adept at doing everything in a big way, I would paint fast and paint prolifically, turning out anywhere from ten to twenty-five images per day. I never thought in terms of a single picture. Once, when I was appearing on *The Hollywood Squares* and the show was being filmed in Florida, I had a huge hotel suite and the whole day to myself, so I just painted my butt off. You see, by then I was beyond the beach age—I didn't want to empty the place by wearing my bikini over an old raincoat.

I was doing the Australian crawl in the grass and Fang said, "Get in the pool." He knows I can't do it in the pool. I learned to do it in the grass. That's where I always do my Australian crawl.

Selling a painting gives me a thrill. It means somebody liked it. Applause is automatic, but when someone buys a picture I think, "Oh, my God." I remember when one lady wandered around an exhibition, looking at my work, and didn't see anything that really took her fancy. Then, just as everyone was leaving, she ran out the door clutching one of my paintings because she loved it so much. Perfectly square, featuring red flowers, and matted in red, it simply spoke to her. That was a major thrill. It's also nice when people who buy my work tell me where it's hanging—"It's hanging above the bed." That's a piece of me, and that's what is so different about this career compared to my other work, which was never properly documented. I have no videos of my symphony performances and only a few videos of my standup routine—most of my work was live, and I love live, but artwork can be touched, felt, and looked at forever.

I express myself through my paintings. Some are funny, some are just plain sweet, but they've all been called feminine and happy, and those are terms I can live with. They're pretty much the story of my life. Painting has proved itself to be a wonderful pastime, especially since a fall in 2002 crushed my right arm. I was trying to make some floor tiles in my loggia look a little cleaner and less old—they *are* old—so I poured Clorox on them, forgot to clean it off, slipped, and collapsed onto my arm, putting all my weight on the elbow. Consequently, I now always need help—I can't do my own hair or put on my panty hose—so while I still paint, the professional piano playing, for instance, is a thing of the past.

No doubt about it, my life is a breeze. But there are times when old age can be a real pain in the ass.

Eleven

THE MADONNA OF
THE GERITOL SET

Don't let that word Madonna bother you. The day I grab my
crotch, that'll mean it's falling off . . . and at my age, it could.

Into my seventies, I was averaging more than 125 club gigs a
year, and what with my work for movies, television, and
cruise lines I was one busy broad. While my material was still
aimed at people of both sexes and all ages, a large part of my audience had grown old with me and could therefore identify with
my evolving persona. Initially, I referred to myself as the Bo
Derek of the Geritol Set. Then, when Bo headed for middle age,
I switched to Madonna. You see, in neither case was I ugly, just
mature. And I always brought my act up to date—the kids who
had been a part of my jokes were now my grandkids.

For me the most embarrassing thing about growing old is when the grandchildren take me to the beach and try to make words out of the veins on my legs—the little bastards. That's why I still take the pill. I don't want any more grandchildren.

Staying active kept me feeling young, and besides, it's what I wanted and what I was accustomed to. I *adored* performing and making people happy, and I enjoyed a perfect setup for quite a few years because the love of my life attended so many of my shows. Bob visited me every weekend when I was working in Reno and he'd join me whenever I was on a cruise. However, after enduring a series of ministrokes—some of which triggered momentary unconsciousness—he was clearly unable to keep this up.

Physically Bob was very frail, and on the last cruise we took together he needed a lot of help from my other guests. So, when I was booked aboard another ship bound for the Caribbean, I talked with his daughter, Suzy, and asked what I should do. She didn't know, and since neither of us had the heart to tell him he couldn't go, Bob and I were soon on our way to the airport. He hadn't slept the night before, and in the morning he couldn't pack his suitcase. That wasn't like him. He wasn't well. Traveling in the limo to LAX, looking totally gray, he put his hand on my knee and said, "You're a good sport." This loving man was dying in front of me, but goddammit, he was determined to make the journey.

We checked-in our cases at the airport, and then, as Bob went to collect his hand luggage after it had passed through the X-ray machine, he leaned over and collapsed. Fortunately, an airline assistant was there with a wheelchair, so we lifted Bob into the chair and took him to the V.I.P. lounge, and by a stroke of sheer luck, Suzy happened to be in town from Memphis. I had no choice but to go on the cruise, so I called her and asked her to collect Bob, and she somehow managed to get him home and up to his bedroom. That was the end. He lived just one day, dying on May 23, 1996, his eighty-sixth birthday. I received a call on board the ship just before performing my show. Heartbroken, I somehow managed to go on. By coincidence it was the last cruise I ever did.

The newlyweds next door were going on a honeymoon cruise and the husband went into a drugstore and bought Dramamine and contraceptives. The dear old druggist took him aside and said, "Son, if it makes you sick, why do you do it?"

Losing the man I was so crazy about created an enormous void in my life, but, as usual, I kept moving forward. Rather than mourn people's passing, I try to celebrate their memory. Death is natural and inevitable. However, over the next few years, my acceptance of this fact was certainly put to the test when I lost two of my children. That isn't the order in which things are supposed to happen. Parents should go first.

Peter, my firstborn, the physical double of his father, who had suffered through Sherwood's nonsense and my own struggles from day one, succumbed to cancer in 1998. He was just fifty-eight. A resident of Venice and one of L.A.'s top county assessors, dealing only with large buildings and hospitals, Peter had smoked his entire adult life, graduating from cigarettes to exotic cigars, yet I didn't even know he was sick until six days before he died. At that point his wife, Bonnie, called to inform me that he was in the hospital, on morphine, and in great pain—but I knew nothing because we hadn't spoken in years. Peter, you see, had more in common with his father than just looks. He, too, had his wires crossed.

As a young kid, he had been cruel to his siblings; the big shot who, when I was away working, would pick on them and force them to do things like drink whiskey. That might sound like a childish prank, but over time he became more and more weird and introverted; extremely bright like Sherwood, yet with a greater ability to function. Intent on getting a proper education rather than just a piece of paper, Peter spent six years at Washington University, where he was a good student and always worked for the school, earning a salary to stay on all summer and handle the new recruits. What's more, he also earned money playing banjo every weekend in Gaslight Square, St. Louis's version of Greenwich Village; and the result was that after graduation he and Bonnie could afford an eighteen-month honeymoon all over Europe.

Ever cautious, the two of them then worked and saved enough money to buy a house, and thereafter they lived frugally, to say the very least. I mean, if you made it into their home you would never see any lampshades, just paper bags on the lamps—that's what I call eccentric. Still, I adored Peter and the two of us were always very close . . . until one Sunday during the early seventies when the camellias were in bloom and Warde and I drove over to his place unannounced. Peter and Bonnie lived in a run-down old bungalow that was situated on a street corner, and when we arrived there, he was watering the lawn with a hose. Well, I opened the car door, leaned out, and he turned the hose on me. My reaction was to get back in the car, close the door, and drive away. That was the last time I ever saw him.

Nothing bad had preceded this incident. Now and again, I'd send Peter $5,000 checks and they'd invariably be returned, cut into paper dolls. I liked that, I thought it was cute, but looking back I now realize he didn't want to be associated with my fame or my celebrity in any way whatsoever. And who could blame him? Fame by association is a dreadful thing because you never know what people really think about *you*, so it's understandable that he'd never allow me to put my name or address on any mail I sent him. I also think he didn't want anyone in his neighborhood to see Warde and me pulling up to the house, so turning the hose on me was probably an act of panic.

Nevertheless, although it wasn't intended to be mean, it sure as hell wasn't normal. My son could have walked up to me and said, "Mother, I don't want people to see you here," and I would have understood. But what he did made little sense at the time, and so I decided to keep out of his way. Clearly, that had been the message. You can't try to reason with people like that. You dance around them. And since this hermitlike creature didn't have a phone—I'm telling you, he and his wife were *primitive*—we stayed in touch by mail, and I never even considered trying to visit him again. I could take a hint.

There was no point in discussing things with Peter because, like so many people with crossed wires, he didn't think he had a problem. And I simply accepted how he felt. It didn't change my love for him. I thought he was terrific. I adored him as always and I was determined to remain positive, so I tried to understand. As far as he was concerned, I was the one who'd broken the rules—I had shown up at his place unannounced. It didn't matter that I wasn't aware those *were* the rules. Every birthday, every holiday I would receive the sweetest cards and loveliest gifts from him, and that's how things remained until the very end. I was accustomed to being surrounded by madness.

Stephanie, my next-to-youngest kid, had been my personal assistant since about 1992, following a stint as a legal secretary. A wonderful human being, she had gone out of her way to please everybody since childhood, smiling at people whenever they looked at her, an absolute vision with her beautiful face and hair like spun gold. Having initially vowed to never work for her mother, she'd then changed her mind during lunch at a Mexican joint when I asked her to replace my majordomo on a trial basis, overseeing a maid, two secretaries, and the gardeners.

Well, baby, you talk about trimming—one by one they were all gone, and soon Stephanie was doing everything they'd been supposed to do. Married to Marv Waldron, with a grown-up son named Michael, she was a hard worker and a brilliant, talented person who read the classics, studied art, loved my artwork, and progressed way beyond me after taking up the piano as an adult. The two of us had so much fun together, I treasured her. And it was also Stephanie who looked out for me during one of the most traumatic periods of my life, when I experienced heart fibrillation one morning in February 1999.

Still very active on stage and screen, I'd provided the voice of the Queen in the Disney animated feature *A Bug's Life* the year before, and I also had a recurring role on CBS's daytime soap *The Bold and the Beautiful*, appearing as Gladys Pope, that nosy, pushy makeup artist who is more bold than beautiful; a feisty old broad, just like me. Oh honey, so many of the characters on that show turn to drink it should be retitled "Benedictine and Brandy." And their bitchery is something else—if, after sex, there's a chalk outline of a body, you know he or she must have been *lousy* in the sack. Still, I love making those guest appearances, and it was just before one such assignment that I experienced rapid and irregular heartbeats. Not that I knew what was going on. I simply felt disoriented.

The hair on the top of my head is so thin, the part is on the roof of my mouth.

Normally, I have someone with me, as I should, but in this case I didn't and I was wandering around the CBS building, totally lost and unable to find my way towards the soundstage. Once there, the show's precious production people rescheduled lunch for later and got my work out of the way so that I could leave and go home. Somehow I managed to get through the shoot, but I didn't feel quite with it and I had a gut feeling something was wrong. When I returned home, I took my pulse and it was dancing: 150. It's supposed to be 72. When it remained at 150 for several hours, I knew I was in trouble. So, as it was now three in the morning and I didn't want to bother Stephanie, I got a cab and went to the emergency room at St. John's in Santa Monica. I should *never* have gone there alone.

In the emergency, I was automatically administered an electric shock to stop the fibrillation, and I could tell by the doctors' reaction that I should have checked in a lot sooner. Next, I was rushed to intensive care and from there a call went out to all the relatives, saying, "We don't think she's going to make it." This were nearly right. While my family made their way to the hospital, I died and was revived by a nurse who gave me mouth-to-mouth before a team administered shocks to the heart. After that, I contracted pneumonia, as well as a bladder infection when a catheter was left in too long, and while the doctors waited for this infection to clear up before inserting a pacemaker, I died twice more. *Code Blue* is what they call it. *Flatlining.* I was in full cardiopulmonary arrest, and if somebody hadn't been around to administer mouth-to-mouth very quickly, that would have been it. Fortunately, I hadn't finished packing my bags for the long trip to nowhere.

Last time I was in the hospital I had Godzilla the nurse. Small animals were trapped in the hair on her legs. She had one eye-

brow that went all the way around her head, and she was so
mean that when flowers arrived she'd say, "Should we unwrap
them or save them for the funeral?" I tried to be friendly with the
woman and make conversation. I said, "What is the difference
between an oral and a rectal thermometer?" She said, "The
taste."

My pacemaker was eventually inserted at the Cedars-Sinai
Medical Center and everything seemed fine, but little did I know
that my real troubles had only just begun. Sitting in a wheelchair
when I was about to be released, I was wheeled into the office of
the top doctor and told him I had a tingling feeling in my tongue
and in my toes. As it turned out, this was the onset of paralysis,
yet I was allowed to leave with assorted drugs and by the time I
got home, I couldn't move. Okay, so I could just about speak, but
otherwise I was an immobile lump. It was, I quickly realized, the
beginning of the end.

Stephanie had to feed me while two nurses were by my side
around the clock: a pair of big, strong dames who were able to
turn me in bed, lift me out, lower me onto the john, wipe me,
you name it. What a job. I was totally helpless, and within a very
short time I knew I didn't want to go through all this. When we
found a new specialist, I asked him about euthanasia and I was
deadly serious. He said, "Well, we're here to save lives, not take
lives." He was so arrogant. No one had any words of reassurance;
words that even *suggested* I might get better. I was just supposed
to exist. Of course, no one at the hospital was willing to ac-

knowledge medical malpractice. I'd been sent home with a drug to regulate my heartbeat and an adverse reaction had caused me to arrive there paralyzed, yet it was as if nothing had happened. Still, litigation was never a part of my thinking. Where would that have gotten me? I just wanted to die.

Stephanie knew the only hope was to contact my old doctor, Fred Lieberman, who used to live in the house across the street and was a close personal friend. Practicing downtown at the St. Vincent Medical Center, he wasn't involved in this mess. He was a precious doctor, an old-fashioned doctor who actually looked at his patient: looked at your face, looked at your palms, looked at your nails. A family doctor. During this time, drinking no alcohol and barely eating, I was down to 90 pounds. The fat was all gone and I was just a prisoner within my own useless body. If only someone would stop my heart beating, I reasoned, the misery would be over. How about contacting "Dr. Death," Jack Kevorkian? The day I considered that little option, he was thrown in jail. Stephanie, however, had other ideas.

She telephoned Fred Lieberman and he made four house calls. During the first, I was sitting in a wheelchair, barely able to speak, and he said, "Give her a martini." That was kind of the turnaround. Fred was zoning in on my despondency. Then he took all of those massive horse pills I'd been sent home with and flushed them down the drain, replacing them with medication that was better suited to my delicate system; my *extremely* delicate system. What's more, since heart-related lung problems were causing wheezing and congestion, he had his assistant come to the house and take chest X-rays. No doubt about it, Fred was the guy who brought me back from the big necropolis. After all I'd gone through with those other doctors, just seeing him gave me hope. And then it was a physical therapist visiting me three times a week for six weeks who helped me to regain movement.

First he started with the fingers and the toes, and after this yielded incredible results, he told me I was ready to try the walker. I'll never forget that moment. After six weeks of paralysis, I didn't have any strength or muscle tone—Stephanie later told me my skin was quite literally hanging on me—so I cried and said I couldn't do it. This therapist, however, *made* me get up and do it, and within seven months I was back onstage, feeling right as rain. The only difference was, with a pacemaker inside me I experienced shortness of breath.

You know you're old when your walker has an air bag . . . and they've discontinued your blood type . . . and your liver spots show through your gloves . . . and your birth certificate is on a scroll . . . and somebody compliments you on your alligator shoes, and you're barefoot . . . and your favorite drink is Metamucil.

Work turned out to be the best tonic, yet this was a weird period for me; a period when death kept rearing its ugly head, and sometimes in the most bizarre circumstances. I mean, how else could I describe a stuation where my limo driver ran over *herself?* That's what happened in Cambridge, Ontario, on May 28, 2001,

when a slender forty-four-year-old woman named Patricia Mar-
cella was navigating a super-stretch Lincoln while I sat in the
back with magician Mercer Helms. He was my opening act as
well as my road manager on this five-venue tour, and for the first
date my manager, Milt Suchin, had booked us into what he
thought would be a swell accommodation: a very chic spa tucked
away deep in the Canadian countryside. In fact, it couldn't have
been worse for our purposes. There was no room service and no
bellboy to help us unload the heavy equipment used in Mercer's
magic act.

You sort of depend on a driver to know where he or she is taking you, but Patricia just couldn't find the place. We were on a
little two-lane road and the spa probably had a small driveway
entrance that she didn't notice. As a result, we went straight past
it, and here we were, eleven o'clock at night, driving around in
the pitch darkness. We were going back and forth, and it's awful
hard to maneuver those huge limos—every time that poor
woman had to turn this thing around on those little two-lane
roads it was a big deal. Finally, she went to get directions, and
when she returned she tried to turn the car around by backing
into a wooded area. However, thanks to all the rain, the wheels
got stuck and then she backed into a tree.

Mercer and I tried to avoid bothering Patricia. She had to be
upset and so we just sat there in silence. Whatever she did was
fine with us. But that's when I saw her get out of the car to look
around. Suddenly realizing it was still in gear and moving backwards, she quickly tried to get back in and was hit by the open
door. I saw her go down as it knocked her under the front of the

vehicle, and I thought, "Oh my God, what's happened?" At the same time, we could have been reversing off a cliff, so while I sat dazed at the back, waiting for the worst, Mercer ran down the full length of the car and jerked the wheel to make it stop. Again it hit a tree, and when Mercer got out he saw Patricia lying on the ground. She was dead, run over by the front wheels. It was the most awful thing I ever witnessed. Now, how to get on with a five-day tour?

Life on the road became more and more tough. With my pacemaker, I wasn't pumping enough oxygen, and that hour of concentrated performing, plus the travel, just got to be too much. I'd reached the point where it was wheelchair time at the airport, and that meant it was over. I thought, "I don't need this." I remember attending one of Frank Sinatra's last concerts where the TelePrompTers said TALK! and I saw Henny Youngman do a show sitting down, reading from cue cards. I wasn't about to put myself in that situation. Still, the hour onstage was actually the tip of iceberg—the traveling and the crowds began to bug me, and I could no longer take having to say hello to the *whole* Indian tribe. Concluding it wasn't worth it, I quit while I was ahead.

A lady went to the doctor and told him one of her breasts was longer than the other. The doctor said, "Well, there's nothing unusual about that. Do you know why?" She said, "Yes, I do. My husband likes to sleep with one of them in his mouth." The doctor said, "Well, there's nothing unusual about that," and she said, "We have twin beds!"

My farewell show took place at the Suncoast Hotel & Casino in Las Vegas on Cinco de Mayo, 2002, and that was just fine with me. I didn't want sadness, I don't entertain it; yet I'd only been retired a few weeks when, in July of that year, my family and my entire being were hit by a bolt out of the blue. Stephanie's husband had five children from a previous marriage, and she visited one of their homes to help plant a garden. She spent the entire morning doing that—she loved to do it and she knew how to do it—but then she said, "I don't feel well," threw up, and decided to lie on the floor in order to save the couch from her dirty clothes. She never got up. Stephanie appeared to fall asleep but she'd suffered a stroke, and from that moment she was brain-dead. She had been so strong and healthy, it took five days for her heart to finally stop beating in the hospital. She was just fifty-three.

I'm so grateful my darling girl didn't suffer, but her passing was the most devastating shock I have ever experienced. The two of us had been incredibly close. Now, essentially, I felt all alone. All alone in my wonderful home that was so full of memories, both good and bad, along with the chattels of a life that now stretched back exactly eighty-five years and had wended its way from the clanging streetcars and surrounding farmland of a small city in early-twentieth-century northwestern Ohio to the sunshine and palm trees of beautiful Southern California, by way of the entire globe; the letters, the photos, the press clippings, the costumes, the artwork . . . and Miss Kitty. Oh, how I *adore* my precious, fluffy, black-and-white Maine Coon cat. I am, you see, a pet lover—animal, insect, you name it.

Back in 1963, during an engagement in Houston, I picked up a jewel-encrusted live Mexican beetle. Able to walk without escaping, thanks to a four-inch chain attached to his rear end, this high-fashion accessory was supposedly all the rage in Paris. I *had* to have one. As it happens, my beetle wasn't at all disturbed by the jewels glued to his back, but he was less than happy with the way I fed him—he died from a lack of water.

A little later, I had a German Shepherd, Kelly, who was a trained watchdog, but when thieves broke into my house, she was in heat and couldn't care less about them stealing a huge diamond ring. Instead, she and a visiting black Labrador were having the time of their lives, producing nine puppies that, when born, formed a perfect arc based on appearances, ranging from pure-bred police dogs to pure-bred labs and all sorts of gradations in between.

In the sixties and seventies I also had a parrot, Pollard, who we called Polly (I can be *so* original). That bird had a large vocabulary. A friend of mine, Stan Kann, had moved from a large house in St. Louis to an apartment in Hollywood, and every afternoon at three o'clock Polly would yell, "Help!"—prompting the neighbors to dial 911. They probably thought someone was being murdered . . . on a daily basis. In the end, my friend had to get rid of his darling parrot, so he gave it to me since I had enough room for him to yell "Help!" without rousing the cops. He was a little troublemaker. One time, when I was practicing for a symphony performance, I recorded Polly interrupting me— I was playing my Beethoven concerto and throughout this beautiful piano music he kept yelling, "Help! Help! Help!"

Able to sing "Silent Night" or just whistle the tune, he could say loads of different words, yet he never spoke in sentences . . . until the day a travel assistant and I were about to fly somewhere, and, as she walked past Polly's cage, he said, "Don't go to the airport." That was the only sentence he'd ever spoken, and he never said it again, but the girl was so spooked she wouldn't take the trip. Still, everybody was *crazy* about Polly, everybody loved him, and he should have lived to about 130. The maid who took care of him was the only person he didn't bite, and she would put him in the courtyard when she cleaned his cage. Well, he chose to eat the house, including some of the paint, and he died of lead poisoning. That was so sad. He was in my will . . .

After Polly passed on, a fan in Canada gave me three Madagascar cockroaches, Manny, Moe, and Jack, which I brought home in my purse. About an inch-and-a-half long, they were quite fat and very cute. And thank God they were all male, because I wouldn't have wanted to put them in a cage and have a whole load of babies escaping. Jack, however, was gay. While Manny and Moe fought like mad, he would sit in the corner. That was smart. They all were. I'd put them on a table and show them to friends, and they would walk to the edge and then walk away. What's more, having grown up in a non-threatening environment, they never ran, they just walked. Friendly and lots of fun, they, too, should have lived much longer, but I didn't know they needed to be fed water very slowly, from something like a wet Kleenex. Consequently, all three died with their heads in the water dish.

Miss Kitty has no such worries. She is pampered, fed, and spoiled. She virtually runs the place. My home is her domain and she even has her own bedroom with a full-sized bed. Oh darling, she tells us *exactly* what she wants. She's a diva cat. I'm just her sidekick, but I wouldn't have it any other way.

"GOODNIGHT, I LOVE YOU . . ."

Some time ago, in my old hometown of Lima, Ohio, the local newspaper wanted to throw a great big bash in my honor. I said, "No." The buildings where I lived are both gone, my school is gone, and so are most of the people I knew, but that's okay. I've outlived *everybody*. And I never look back.

Down the years I've received quite a few awards, and among those that have given me the biggest thrill are the Comedy Lifetime Achievement Award, which I donated to the Smithsonian Institution, and the Photoplay Award, which was earned by way of readers' votes. I treasure that. And I also appreciate my star on the Hollywood Walk of Fame because that is forever, just like the one in Palm Springs. In St. Louis, I have a park bench.

My kids, meanwhile, all lead very different lives. Sally, in her horrible schizoid condition, is still incredibly sweet; a sweet little lady who's just *way* out. She won't let anyone wash her, she makes strange, disjointed sounds, and, when you speak with her, she hears other "voices" and talks to them. It's so tragic. For years, Stephanie and Suzanne visited her frequently, and to this day Suzy still sees her every month, bringing her things and taking her for rides in the car.

Suzy is an accomplished equestrian and qualified therapist. Her son, Paul, is my eldest grandchild, followed by Stephanie's son, Michael. My own youngest kid, Perry, used to be the biggest escrow officer in California—he had five offices until the market went belly-up—but now he's a banker and doing *very* well, living in the Valley with his wife, Julia, and their kids, Christopher and Cory.

We Californians are constantly accused of not having seasons, but we do. We have fire, flood, mud, and drought. Who can forget that six-year drought? A tree went up to a dog. And then, when it rains too hard, it's bad news. It's a terrible thing to be on your way to the airport and your house passes you. The last time we had one of those downpours, a flasher opened his raincoat and caught a trout.

When people find me funny I adore it. And when they re-member a line from forty years ago that I've forgotten, it's a major thrill. Clearly, they were paying close attention. I've played to huge crowds and millions of folks since the start of my career, but I always feel great when an individual compliments my work. I still make the occasional live appearance, and I enjoy regular assignments on the big and small screens, including recurring roles on the TV soap *The Bold and the Beautiful* and *7th Heaven*. They write me in whenever they find a place for me, especially if there's a wedding. That's when they need more faces. I'm written in when there's a wedding on *any* show.

Whereas some people are into spreading gloom, my business is happiness. All of my letters, for as long as I can remember, have been signed "Love," regardless of who they're addressed to. For me, love *is* the answer, and I hear that word applied to me all the time, no matter where I am or who is saying it: "I love you," "My mother loves you," "My grandmother loves you," "*We* love you." They constantly use that word. Never mind those who say, "You're my biggest fan!" *Am I?* Or "I remember you and your cigarette lighter!" *Lighter?* That's just a case of people feeling nervous and getting all discombobulated.

As a child I had very strong passions and aspirations, and I've lived to realize them all. I've had a family, I've known great romance, clothes are coming out of my ears, God only knows the friends I have, and although I didn't foresee all the travel, it has been just incredible. I was the kid who never had a room or a birthday party. All I had to play with were boxes, but I *loved* my boxes. The glass, you see, is always half-full, and I'm grateful for all I've experienced.

I don't miss being on the road. I'm really well adjusted. Some performers don't have another life, but I've had eighteen other lives and still have eighteen more. I have many interests, including art and ecology, and I'm always busy and never bored. I'm out for dinner every night, the eternal guest, and I always have a new beau on my arm, so this is a great time. It's the harvest. I plowed the field and planted the seeds, and now I'm watching the flowers grow. It's a time of life that should really be nice, and mine *really* is.

Sure, I've experienced my fair share of unhappiness, but throughout the years I've always tried to express and give cheer. One of my earliest memories is of standing as a teenie little kid in Sunday school, singing a hymn whose words still resonate in my ears:

> *Brighten the corner where you are!*
> *Brighten the corner where you are!*
> *Someone far from harbor you may guide across the bar;*
> *Brighten the corner where you are!*

I bought that. And I sold it.

Acknowledgments

I am eternally grateful to Linda Konner for introducing me to Richard Buskin, an extraordinarily brilliant writer, a raconteur and gentleman, without whom there would be no book.

And I thank Linda for selling it to my dear old friend Jeremy Tarcher.

About the Authors

PHYLLIS DILLER, the world's first and foremost female standup comic, has been entertaining audiences for five decades with her groundbreaking, often self-penned material, zany appearance, trademark laugh, and countless stage, film, and television performances. An accomplished painter, Phyllis has also appeared as a piano soloist with more than one hundred symphony orchestras in the United States and Canada. She lives in Brentwood, California.

RICHARD BUSKIN is the *New York Times* best-selling author of more than a dozen books, on subjects ranging from Marilyn Monroe and Princess Diana to The Beatles and Sheryl Crow. His articles have appeared in newspapers such as the *New York Post, The Sydney Morning Herald, The Observer,* and *The Independent,* and he also writes features and reviews for film and music magazines around the world. A native of London, England, he lives in Chicago, Illinois.